Kids Are Still Saying the Darndest Things

How to Order:

Single copies may be ordered from Prima Publishing, P.O. Box 1260BK, Rocklin, CA 95677; telephone (916) 786-0426. Quantity discounts are also available. On your letterhead, include information concerning the intended use of the books and the number of books you wish to purchase.

Kids Are Still Saying the Darndest Things

Dandi Daley Mackall

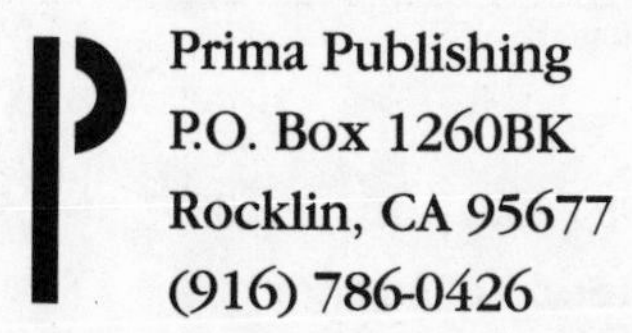

Prima Publishing
P.O. Box 1260BK
Rocklin, CA 95677
(916) 786-0426

Production by Melanie Field, Bookman Productions
Copyediting by Karen Stough
Composition by Janet Hansen, Alphatype
Interior design by Judith Levinson
Cover jacket design by The Dunlavey Studio, Sacramento

Library of Congress Cataloging-in-Publication Data

Mackall, Dandi Daley.
Kids are still saying the darndest things / by Dandi Daley Mackall.
p. cm.
Includes index.
ISBN 1-55958-352-5
1. Children—Quotations. I. Title.
PN6328.C5M25 1993
818'.54020809282—dc20 93-1715
CIP

94 95 96 97 98 RRD 10 9 8 7 6 5 4 3 2 1

Printed in the United States of America

To my loving and much loved husband, Joe,

who also says the darndest things.

Thanks, honey—for everything.

Contents

Foreword

As I cross the country lecturing, people who have seen me interview kids on TV or who have read my "kid" books invariably ask me one question: How have kids changed in the last 40 years? And the answer, surprisingly, in this world of constant change, is *not at all.* Of course I am talking about kids under 10, an age when they are still unaffected by the woes of the world and the trash talk of teenagers. Their world is still framed by their home life, the example of their parents, and their first encounters with their peers. This opinion has been delightfully reinforced by this new book, *Kids Are Still Saying the Darndest Things,* put together lovingly by Dandi Daley Mackall almost 40 years after my own book *Kids Say the Darndest Things* became the #1 bestseller in the nation. Dandi has captured the wonderful, wacky world of the guileless child with her anecdotes and quotations from today's small fry. My advice is: open this book to any page and enjoy, enjoy, enjoy!

Art Linkletter

Preface

About thirty-five years ago, Art Linkletter wrote a book that highlighted his TV and career interviews with children from all over America. Four million readers have read and laughed over *Kids Say the Darndest Things.*

I remember reading as a child what my peers had to say in that book. What a great idea, I thought, to let us have a say for a change, to allow children to talk while grown-ups listen!

Now that I'm the grown-up with my own children, it's still a great idea. Kids are still saying the darndest things. We have a new generation of kids; it's time for them to have their own book.

I've been interviewing children across America, listening to their child-wisdom. I've gathered stories from parents, grandparents, teachers, anyone who has taken the time to hear what kids are saying. In many ways, young children haven't changed. They still fight with their brothers and sisters. "I don't mind sharing," announced my own six-year-old, ". . . unless it's my stuff." Children are still blessed with imaginations far beyond our reach: "Heaven? That's where your cat evaporates when it dies."

But times have changed—and, in many ways, so have kids. I met first-graders who talked about their fear of AIDS. Many of the inner-city kids I talked with had faced drug problems and gang pressures by the time they turned nine. "The hardest part about being a kid," said one eight-year-old girl, "is saying 'No, Home-boy! I don't want to try your drugs!' "

But she does say no to drugs. And even though some of what kids are saying reveals problems, changes we wish kids didn't have to face in their world, the children themselves are wonderful, honest, and inspiring.

Despite the differences in the two generations, children of Art Linkletter's era and children of today are kindred spirits, linked through the mystical gift of childhood. "I would like to be a dog," a four year old confided in me, "because I like to bark. And when I'm people, my teacher gets me in trouble for barking." "I'd be a snake," a little boy told Art Linkletter years ago, "so I could poison our teacher." No adult can predict what may come from the mouths of babes in any generation.

Mr. Linkletter concluded his delightful book with the following:

> There's a vast gulf between the world of children and our own. And every time we bridge that gulf—even if it's only for a moment—we recapture some of the fresh-ness and spontaneity that make life worth living.*

*Art Linkletter, *Kids Say the Darndest Things!* (Englewood Cliffs, N.J.: Prentice-Hall, Inc., 1957).

The gulf between grown-ups and children is still there. Freshness and un-*adult*-erated spontaneity still reign in the world of children. In this book, in their own words, kids invite us to catch a glimpse, a vision of their world.

Acknowledgments

My thanks to all the parents and grandparents and teachers who shared their kids with me. And most of all, thanks to all the kids who let me peek into their world. This is your book, guys.

✸ *CHAPTER 1* ✸

Home Sweet Home

My mother had a great deal of trouble with me, but I think she enjoyed it.—Mark Twain

Four-year-old Jenny came home in tears from preschool. "Christopher says he's rich and we're poor because he lives in a house, and we only live in a 'partment. We do *not* live in a 'partment, do we, Mommy? We live in a home!"

Most kids still believe there's no place like home. And plenty of little girls still think a mom is a pretty great thing to be.

Question: Why do you want to be a mom?

❖❖❖ "Because they know everything."

❖❖❖ "Because they have kids."

❖❖❖ "Because they dress up and look beautiful."

❖❖❖ "Because they don't have to do anything."

❖❖❖ "Because they can boss kids *and* grown-ups, and dads can only boss kids."

❖❖❖ "Because mothers can make as much money as daddies, but they get to spend more."

❖❖❖ "I'd like to be a mother because I'd like to be the one who decides what's for dinner."

❖❖❖ "I want to be a mom because I like little babies . . . and kids . . . and daddies."

Katy conceded that she did want to be a mother and that she wanted ten children. "But I'm having the five girls in my tummy, and their daddy's having the five boys in his tummy. That's more fair and square."

Question: What's a mom?

❖❖❖ "Someone who loves you, even when you're grumpy—and even when *she's* grumpy."

❖❖❖ "A mom is the one who's gotta vacuum when the company's coming over."

❖❖❖ "A mom goes out on dates—with your dad."

❖❖❖ "Moms are people who make kids do stuff—like rooms and teeth."

When I asked kindergartners and first-graders to describe their moms, their answers conjured up some interesting visions.

Question: How would I recognize your mom if I saw her?

❖❖❖ "She wears long fingernails and a yellow sweater, and stays inside."

❖❖❖ "My mom has long hair that's yellow on the bottom and white in the middle and black on the top."

❖❖❖ "You'd recognize my mom because she looks eighteen, but she's really twenty-four."

❖❖❖ "My mother's a stockbreaker, and you can always tell a stockbreaker because they're the ones who bring home lots of toys and presents."

❖❖❖ "Curly brown hair, brown eyes, glasses," then in a whisper, "and she's kinda chubby."

❖❖❖ "My mom wears big clothes—big jeans and big sweats."

❖❖❖ "You could always tell it's my mom," said a little blonde gal with a proud grin, "because she would wave at you."

❖❖❖ "My mom has red hair and eyes, and she washes her hair before she goes to church."

Jennifer talked a blue streak to Papa as they walked along together. "See these ants, Papa? They have one queen and no king. He couldn't stand being bossed around."

Father attempted to teach his three-year-old son about relationships. He had covered grandparents, uncles, aunts, and cousins. Now it was time for a quiz. "Brian," said his father, "when you grow up and get married and have a baby, what will that make me?"

Without any hesitation Brian replied, "Happy."

Question: What does your dad look like?

❖❖❖ "Black hair with a bald spot in it, glasses, a silver ring, and usually dirty."

❖❖❖ "My dad has black-brown hair, two eyes, wears a tan hat, tan overalls, tan shoes, and he's a little plumpy."

❖❖❖ "Oh, you couldn't miss my dad. He's one-half fat, one-half skinny, and if you say 'Mark,' he'll turn around."

❖❖❖ "My dad is old and he has this place on the top of his head where he won't let any hair grow at all."

"Why is that?" I queried.

"So no birds will land and build their nests there," she answered. "But he takes this one long hair and combs it all the way over to the other side of his head to make up for it."

❖❖❖ "Well, you wouldn't recognize my dad from his picture."

"Why not?"

"Because the picture was taken when he still had ribs."

Question: What does your dad do all day?

❖❖❖ "Makes law."

❖❖❖ "He travels. He knows every road in the whole world."

❖❖❖ "Dad works all day and then farms all night. He doesn't play with kids."

❖❖❖ "My dad gets dirty outside all day and gets his skin real brown."

❖❖❖ "He sits in his office all day—so nobody else gets it."

❖❖❖ "My dad teaches at the university and yells at other people's kids during the day."

❖❖❖ "He sits down all day, and he makes more money than when he had to stand up all day."

❖❖❖ "My dad's a prestidigitator."

"What's that?"

"I don't know. I think he sells elevators."

❖❖❖ "I don't know what my dad does. He just won't tell us."

Question: What would you change about your dad?

❖❖❖ "I'd have him stay home and not fix things."

❖❖❖ "I'd make him play Sky Commandos with me—just once, anyway."

❖❖❖ "I'd change his looks—spike his hair, give him nice work clothes and weird boots."

❖❖❖ "Put hair on his bald spot."

❖❖❖ "I'd change his attitude—make him nice, and not mean."

❖❖❖ "Change his back, so it wouldn't hurt him all the time."

❖❖❖ "Make him happy."

Question: How did your mom and dad meet?

❖❖❖ "My dad was standing outside a department store window, and he was staring in at a leather belt with a shiny gold belt buckle. My mom saw him standing there and thought he was pretty cute because he still had hair then. So, she went over to the window and kind of scooched in next to him. Dad told her that if she would buy him that belt buckle, he would marry her. She did, and he did, and here I am."

❖❖❖ "Oh, I don't think my mom and dad ever met each other."

❖❖❖ "Oh, they just went to the same restaurant. That's all," said one third-grade girl.

❖❖❖ "My mom and dad met in a bar and got married," said her classmate.

❖❖❖ "My dad was really looking for another Patricia. He got his friend to set him up with her, but he ended up with the wrong Patricia and married her."

❖❖❖ But one girl was proud that she knew the whole story of her parents' courtship. "My dad was my mom's teacher. So she wrote in her assignment that she thought he was cuter than any of the other teachers. So they got married."

❖❖❖ "My mom got herself a spell book and put a spell on him," Tony told me.

"How did she do it?"

"You just say some certain words and sprinkle vinegar on them."

❖❖❖ "My parents met in the backseat of my dad's car."

❖❖❖ "My mom was learning to be a writer and taking a class on how to write murder mysteries. My dad saw her and thought she was pretty and asked her what was her favorite way to kill people. And the next day they got married."

Question: What do your mom and dad do all day?

❖❖❖ "Dad works. I don't know what mom does."

❖❖❖ "They baby-sit at McDonald's."

❖❖❖ "My mom makes more money than my dad," one girl proudly told us. "And my dad sweats more."

❖❖❖ "Mom goes to the barn in the morning, calls people all afternoon, and goes to the bank. My dad is just gone all day."

❖❖❖ "Mom cleans the house every day, cleans the dishes, runs errands, and does my homework on the computer."

❖❖❖ "My mom talks on the phone in the morning, and in the afternoon she coin collects."

❖❖❖ "My dad cooks breakfast," Hannah told us.

"That's nice," I said. "What did he cook this morning?"

"He didn't. My mom cooked breakfast this morning."

"I see. What did your mother cook for your breakfast this morning?" I tried.

"Cereal," Hannah answered.

"And what does your dad cook when he cooks your breakfast?"

"I don't know. He always sleeps in."

Now I was really confused. "I thought you said your dad usually cooks breakfast."

"Well," she said a bit defensively, "he would if he didn't sleep in so much."

❖❖❖ "My mom raises horses," said a kindergartner. "And my dad works in a glue factory."

I didn't touch that one.

If you can't fight family, whom can you fight?

Question: Does everybody get along well with each other in your family?

❖❖❖ "Are you kidding?" asked Tosha, a bright-eyed, thin first-grader. "We all fight with Daddy."

"Why is that?"

" 'Cause whenever one of us leaves a piece of candy on the table, or on our dressers, or anywhere, Daddy eats it."

❖❖❖ "Whenever my mom gets mad at us," said Bev, "she chases us all around the house with a remote control. She says she going to change us into good children."

❖❖❖ "We're kind of worried about my dad," said a serious eight-year-old from Pennsylvania. "Usually he comes home every night after working all day, and he's tired and grouchy. But the last two nights, he's come home and told jokes."

"That sounds serious," I agreed. "What do you think it means?"

"I don't know," he said, shaking his head, "but it's something up to no good."

❖❖❖ "My mom causes most of the fights in our house."

"How?"

"She throws her clothes around, even her brassiere."

❖❖❖ "My mother and daddy sit around all day and make fun of people."

❖❖❖ "Mom and Dad fight a lot," six-year-old Margaret confessed.

"Do you take sides?" I asked.

"I always stick with mom because she lets me get away with murder."

❖❖❖ "My parents fight over how much money to give me for doing my homework. I pretty much stay out of it."

Bill Cosby hints at the inevitable sibling rivalry when he says, "People who have only one child, don't have kids."

One six-year-old confided, "I don't know why I hate it so much when my mom yells at me, but I really like it when she yells at my sisters."

Mom and David were sitting on the bed, immersed in a game of Candyland, when all of a sudden little sister Jackie's cry signaled the end of her naptime.

Mom: "Oops, I better go to Jackie."
David: "No, I didn't hear anything."
Jackie cried again, this time much louder.
David: "I didn't hear anything again."

Casey, age three, waited with his grandmother to meet his new baby brother. As the car bearing the bundle of joy pulled into the driveway, Casey warned grandma, "I don't want no grandmas holding no babies!"

Question: What do your brothers and sisters do?

❖❖❖ "My li'l brother sits on Mommy's lap all day long. Then there's no room for me. And if I try to sit on the floor by them, he kicks me in the head and my mommy laughs."

❖❖❖ "My baby sister bawls *all* day. She even bawls all night when she's asleep—only more quieter."

❖❖❖ "My big brother gets to go wherever he wants to go, and it makes me very mad because I can't go everywhere he wants to go. But when he *is* home, all he does is hit me, so I guess it's better to have him go everywhere."

❖❖❖ "My brother holds his hand over my mouth so I can't talk."

❖❖❖ "My brother and sister take turns lifting me up off the floor."

"That sounds like fun," I remarked.

"Well, it's not," came the reply. "They lift me by my neck."

❖❖❖ "When we have soup, my sister eats mine. And if I won't let her, she dumps it on me."

❖❖❖ "My sister and I have fun jumping on the bed and doing tricks on it. It's fun until she pushes me off the bed and I land hard on the floor. That's the only part I don't like."

"Why do you think she does that?" I inquired.

"She says she just pushes me off the bed, and if I land on the floor, it's my fault."

❖❖❖ "My brother kicks me whenever he feels like it."

"Why?" I asked sympathetically.

"Because I'm cuter than he is, and he's bigger than I am."

❖❖❖ "My sister agitates me," pronounced a curly-haired kindergartner.

"What does that mean?" I asked.

"Agitate means you take someone else's candy and toys."

❖❖❖ "Me and my brother are twins," said Guillermo.

"That must be fun," I said.

"We look just alike, but I was born first, and he was born second."

"When's your birthday?"

"Mine is December 10, and his is March."

"Wait a minute," I said. "I thought you said you were twins."

"We are," he assured me. "We have the same hair color and the same exact pair of shoes."

Question: How do you get along with your brothers and sisters?

❖❖❖ "I have eight brothers and five sisters," said a tired-looking nine-year-old. "How do you think I get along?"

"Which of you causes the most trouble?" I asked.

"Chuckie," she replied without hesitation. "He bites like a dog, and he gave us all chicken pox!"

❖❖❖ "My sister and I can't get along. We try to outdo each other."

"Give me an example."

"If my mom hugs my sister, I cry. Then when my mother hugs me, my sister tries to cry harder than I did."

❖❖❖ "My sister causes all kinds of trouble."

"What does she do?"

"She's only two years old, and she goes around telling everybody she's five or ten."

❖❖❖ "My brother hits himself in the head with a pipe. Then he hits his head into the wall. And when he gets tired of that, he takes a cooking pot and throws it at my head."

"Why does he do that?" I asked with concern.

"For fun. You should see him when he's mean!"

❖❖❖ "My brother, he likes to scare my pregnant sister all the time. He likes to catch her lying down. Then he tries to jump over her belly."

❖❖❖ "My brother is weird. He likes to jump on the bed."

"That doesn't sound too bad," I said.

"He's eighteen!"

❖❖❖ "My sister's really funny," said Paula. Then she thought a minute, and amended her evaluation. "Except when she tries to break the baby in little pieces."

❖❖❖ "My little brother likes to pet fish and put lipstick on them and stuff. We go through a lot of fish."

❖❖❖ "My big brother gets on my nerves," announced a first-grade girl.

"How does he do that?" I asked.

"He kicks me and bites me and punches me and beats me up." She sighed deeply. "He really gets on my nerves."

❖❖❖ "I have four sisters," said David, a dejected kindergartner. "And they all spit on me and laugh."

❖❖❖ "My brother marks on the walls."

"What do your parents do?"

"We move."

❖❖❖ "My brother is salt!" said a second-grade girl.

"I don't understand," I said. "What does *salt* mean?"

"It means my brother is stupid, but I'm not allowed to tell anybody my brother is stupid."

❖❖❖ "My brother is so mean. He writes 'Kick' on your back, and then he kicks you. And he punches you without even writing it first."

Question: Why do you think you have brothers and sisters?

❖❖❖ "Good question!"

❖❖❖ "A kid needs someone to play trucks with."

❖❖❖ "You gotta have big brothers and sisters so when your mom and dad leave you at home and go do something fun, you're not home alone."

❖❖❖ "So you learn to share . . . the hard way."

Extended families didn't come up as often in my visits with schoolchildren as they seem to when Art Linkletter conducted his visits a generation ago. But many of today's children still stand in awe of that unique uncle or aunt or cousin.

Seven-year-old Luke was wearing a white shirt, black tie, dress pants, and good shoes when I visited his first-grade class. "My uncle wears fake clothes whenever he comes over to our house," he confided.

"Fake clothes?" I asked. "What are fake clothes?"

"A fine suit and tie, expensive shoes, leather belt, and stuff to make him smell good."

"How are those things fake?" I asked, still puzzled.

"We all know his real clothes are dirty jeans and a raggy T-shirt, and we know what he really smells like."

Martin looked tired when he and some of his classmates met me in a Chicago school library.

"My cousin lives with us now, and he's cried for four months without stopping," he told us.

"Are you sure he hasn't stopped crying in four months?" I asked.

"I'm sure!" said Martin. "And you can ask my mom if you don't believe me."

"Why does he cry so much?"

"He wants to have all the attention so I can't have any of it."

Question: Do you have any weird relatives, aunts, uncles, et cetera?

❖❖❖ "I have a voodoo aunt who can put a spell on you so that fourteen years later you're still getting sick and tired."

❖❖❖ "I got me a godsister who ought not be a godsister because she be making up jokes that there's no way God's gonna like."

❖❖❖ "My uncle got his tooth knocked out, and it grew back gold!"

❖❖❖ "My dad's mother, my grandmother, can laugh like a real witch and my mother says she is one."

Families with stepparents and stepchildren are no longer the exception.

"How many brothers and sisters do you have?" I asked a first-grade girl.

"I have one sister who's real. Then I have a brother who's really a half brother, but he lives with us so he's like a real too. Then I have two more half brothers who I almost never see because they don't live here and because they're old. So, how many is that?"

For most kids, pets are part of the family.

Question: Tell me about your pets.

❖❖❖ "I have two dogs that aren't funny."

"What do you mean?" I asked.

"I got one dog, but he runned away. Then I got another dog, and he runned away too. Now, didn't I tell you they weren't funny?"

❖❖❖ "I have a new baby cat that meows at birds and wrestles dogs."

❖❖❖ "We have a cat named Silence who is fifty pet years old and he knows how to get carsick every time he rides in our good car, and sometimes when he doesn't."

❖❖❖ "We have a cat and a dog. And whenever the cat sees the dog, the cat pukes. And the dog is so grossed out, he leaves her alone."

❖❖❖ "I have a turtle, a dog, a rabbit, a fish, a lizard, and a snake," said a six-year-old boy with big, brown eyes.

"Which one is the most interesting?" I quizzed.

"Jordan, my lizard. He's the only one at my house who eats screaming mice."

❖❖❖ "My piranha ate my goldfish . . . and—," he added when his fellow third-graders didn't look impressed, "—my cousin's hand."

❖❖❖ "My dog could ride a horse," Melody told us.

"Like in a circus?" I asked.

"Probably," she answered. "So far he only rides arms."

❖❖❖ "I have a black cat named Rusty, but my grandpa calls her Orangey just to make me mad."

❖❖❖ "My cat is the smartest cat in the world. He knows how to call birds for dinner."

❖❖❖ "I have a little black dog named Spike who is so smart, he's got me and my two brothers each thinking he likes us best."

❖❖❖ "I have a parrot who married our dog. But they don't do anything interesting, and he can't get her to talk."

❖❖❖ "I have six seals, and they're all named Katy."

❖❖❖ Six-year-old Wendy told us, "My cat is a real stinker!"

"What do you mean?" I asked.

"She knocks at the back door, and before we can answer it, she runs away."

❖❖❖ "My dog can do tricks, and he's not an old dog," Mick said proudly.

"Did you teach your dog any tricks?"

"Yep," Mick said, glancing around the room to make sure as many children as possible would hear. "He's only ten months old, and I already taught him to walk upstairs."

"How about coming downstairs?" I pressed.

Mick looked irritated by the question. "Maybe next year."

❖❖❖ "A Japanese fighting fish, a cricket, three snails—and a spider. But don't tell my mom about the spider. It's a secret."

Tracy's Uncle Jack loved animals. Before Tracy was born, Uncle Jack had a wonderful beagle named Bucky. Bucky died, but his exploits lived on after him; time and time again, Uncle Jack would bring up Bucky's colorful history.

"I remember when Bucky was a puppy and had to sleep on the foot of my bed." Or, "Ol' Bucky used to love ice cream." Or, "I used to take Bucky along on my fishing trips."

Finally, when Tracy was four years old, she looked Uncle Jack straight in the eyes as he began another

Bucky story: "Uncle Jack, you ought to get yourself a dog that isn't dead."

From Anne, contemplating the neighbor's dog: "I think I know what makes dogs different from people. This dog doesn't know he's a dog. But I know I'm a people."

✸ *CHAPTER 2* ✸

Heaven and Hell

Let the children come to me, for the Kingdom of God belongs to such as they.—The Bible, Mark 10:14

When I asked kindergartners and first-graders their thoughts about God, they were ready with quick answers.

Question: What does God look like?

❖❖❖ "He's really cute—and nice, and wears blue and white clothes."

❖❖❖ "He's plastic. You can see right through him."

❖❖❖ "He wears a blue cape over a white cape, with brown shoes."

❖❖❖ "Well, God has this giant beard, and black and brown hair, big eyes, really big hands, huge feet; but his ears are as little as mine."

❖❖❖ "He's invisible. That means he can turn into anything he wants—even a baby, or a big daddy, or a frog, or a snake."

❖❖❖ "He's very, very, very tall so he can look over everybody's head and see what even little kids are up to."

❖❖❖ "He's big and strong and made of wood."

❖❖❖ "He carries a big pouch over his shoulders."

❖❖❖ One little girl contended, "He never wears clothes."

Several of her peers at the table where we sat tried to set her straight, but she wouldn't give in. Finally she offered a compromise: "Only on Sundays, then he wears his underwear."

❖❖❖❖❖❖

At one inner-city school, several second-graders got into a lively discussion about God.

"He's got white cloth all over his body," said one little girl, Marissa, "and he lives all the way up."

"No sir!" said Earl.

"Yes," she continued, "all the way up in a cloud."

"That's crazy talk!" Earl insisted.

But Marissa was calm and sure. "And he's white, and has blond hair and a mustache," she almost whispered, with a knowing air.

Earl was incensed. "He's all different colors—black, brown, white, red—"

"He's not red," Albert said, joining the group. "The devil's red, with a red-hot fork."

"He changes colors, though—God does," said another second-grade girl, Amelia. "Like sometimes he's white, sometimes black, sometimes Puerto Rican, sometimes Chinese, and stuff like that."

"God's real old and has bags under his eyes," said a first-grade girl.

"Yeah, he real old!" agreed her friend.

"He gets them bags because he stay up all night to watch over us and care about us."

"God has wings," added a little boy who had been trying to get the attention of his two female classmates all day. But they continued to ignore him and his revelation about wings. He sighed, sank in his chair, and told me, "I guess everybody already knows that."

Everyone marveled at Michele's understanding as she belted out the song "Jesus Is a Bridge over Troubled Water"—until they really listened to her words: "Jesus Is a Bridge over a Tub of Water." Later Michele could be heard singing another revised favorite: "Jesus loves the little children of the world / red and yellow, black and white / all are precious in his sight / . . . except NOT YOU GUYS!"

When Molly was four she surprised her mother with a serious question: "Mommy, is God made of human?"

Question: What is heaven like?

❖❖❖ "It's like hell, with clouds."

❖❖❖ One little boy slapped the table in front of him and declared, "It's the greatest!"

❖❖❖ "Heaven's pretty, with pretty angels. And all the beds have gold sheets . . . with no holes in them."

❖❖❖ "Mickey Mouse will be there!" shouted one little girl. When I expressed surprise, she explained, "Didn't you hear? Walt Disney died."

❖❖❖ "It's a cloud house with no roof."

❖❖❖ "Nobody there ever washes. There's no dirt!"

❖❖❖ "It's dark and very close to the moon."

❖❖❖ "There are books everywhere—lots and lots of books." Then, for my edification, "God likes to read, you know."

❖❖❖ "In heaven, people don't fight or eat each other."

❖❖❖ "Do you know what?" expanded one little girl. "In heaven it's always shiniest when it's raining and ugly on earth."

❖❖❖ "Heaven is in the air, right between cool and warm."

❖❖❖ "It's like playing in my attic and sitting on the white fluffy stuff—you know, the installation to keep your house warm. Only in heaven, nobody has to go down to the bathroom."

Not everyone was convinced that heaven would be the ideal place to go.

❖❖❖ "Heaven is a big town where people turn into skeletons."

❖❖❖ "It's foggy, with stairs, and you can see ghosts."

❖❖❖ "There's a bunch of dead people there. Yuck!"

❖❖❖ My favorite definition of heaven came from a six-year-old, brown-eyed beauty: "Heaven is where your cat evaporates when it dies."

Little Chris was playing cowboys with his aunt when she pointed a toy gun at him and said, "I've got you covered, buster. Raise your hands. And say your prayers, pardner."

Chris, an astonished look on his face, raised his hands in the air and said, "God is great. God is good. Thank you, Jesus, for this food. Amen."

During a quiet moment in church, Mother looked over to find six-year-old Megan staring at the wall hanging of Jesus on the cross. Megan stretched out her arms and held her head to the side. "Gosh," she exclaimed. "I bet that hurt!"

Question: What do you do in heaven?

❖❖❖ "You can do anything you want, silly!"

❖❖❖ "You eat candy, and don't get fat or cavities."

❖❖❖ "You play with Play-doh and make stuff out of cardboard."

❖❖❖ "You can buy toys without money because heaven money is invisible and it looks like everybody has the same amount."

❖❖❖ "You water-skate all day long!" declared one squirmy first-grader.

"What's water-skating?" I asked innocently.

He smiled slyly and replied, "You'll find out."

❖❖❖ "You can stay up all day and all night, and your parents can't make you go to bed because there aren't any—beds. There *are* parents."

❖❖❖ "In heaven you make stuff out of staples."

❖❖❖ "In heaven, everybody helps everybody all day long. And you don't even get tired."

❖❖❖ "You can hug God—and Grandpa and Grandma."

❖❖❖ "In heaven, nobody's hungry or thirsty because everybody eats bread all day long, and drinks blood that tastes like grape juice."

❖❖❖ "You help people on earth be smarter."

And there were a few dissenters who weren't quite so sure heavenly activity would be so . . . heavenly.

❖❖❖ "You play the harp all day, whether you like it or not."

❖❖❖ "You have to paint clouds."

❖❖❖ "Most of the time you try to get dry because it seems like it's always raining in heaven."

One day Rebecca explained to her grandmother, "Grandma, we come from heaven, where God made us. And we go back to heaven when we die. So our time here on earth must be our vacation."

Question: *How do you get to heaven?*

❖❖❖ "God magic."

❖❖❖ "You go to hell and turn right."

❖❖❖ "On a trampoline."

❖❖❖ "You get to heaven by getting the bad spanked out of you."

❖❖❖ "You get there," said one little girl, pointing up, "the same way you got down here."

❖❖❖ "Nobody seems to know."

❖❖❖ More than one child had decided you must fly to get to heaven. Alan was more specific: "You fly. It takes three days to get there . . . nonstop."

Some of the young philosophers had apparently given considerable thought to entering heaven.

❖❖❖ "You leave your bones in the ground to turn into dirt, and you send your heart ahead to heaven."

❖❖❖ "First, you gotta turn into a spirit. From there, it's easy!"

❖❖❖ "You give God a hug. But he's invisible, so you fall right through him and land in heaven."

❖❖❖ "Be good, and be buried."

❖❖❖ "You can die, or you can love God. If you decide to love God, you don't have to die first . . . I think."

❖❖❖ "Somebody drives you there in a big, black limousine."

Question: ***What's hell like?***

❖❖❖ "It's where the devil whips you until your teeth fall out."

❖❖❖ "It's like a big hot tub."

❖❖❖ "Where you get slapped around and they put fire on you."

❖❖❖ Another little boy informed me, "It's where you go if you live in California."

"Will everybody in California go to hell?" I asked, alarmed.

"No, just the ones who fall between the cracks during earthquakes."

❖❖❖ "Hell's where you're going if you ain't goin' up."

❖❖❖ "The devil lives there, and he's mean and red, and on a team called the demons."

❖❖❖ "It's where the devil turns people into skeletons—whether they want to be turned into skeletons or not."

❖❖❖ "Hell's where you go when you pout."

❖❖❖ "Little pieces of ice," answered one little Oklahoman.

"Little pieces of ice?" I repeated.

"Yeah, little pieces of ice. I think they fall down from Mars."

Because of the lateness of the hour, I had to let that one pass. It wasn't until later that night when I was copying my notes that I finally understood. In Oklahoma, *hell* sounds like *hail*.

✸ *CHAPTER 3* ✸

Happy Holidays

Home is the place where, when you have to go there, / They have to take you in.—Robert Frost

When I polled six- to eight-year-olds to discover their favorite holiday, Christmas came in first.

Question: Why do you like Christmas so much?

❖❖❖ "You don't go to school for a long time at Christmas. You just get up early and stay in the same pajamas all day and all night for weeks."

❖❖❖ "Everybody sings songs at Christmas, and nobody yells at you when you don't know the words."

❖❖❖ "It's the only holiday Santa Claus celebrates."

❖❖❖ "I like Christmas best because it's when we hunt in the attic for stuff and light up the world."

❖❖❖ Seven-year-old Jenny had a problem with Christmas.

"What I want to know is, does God have fingers?"

Treading carefully, I answered her question with a question: "Why do you want to know?"

"Because, since it's his birthday and all, I wanted to give him a present, but I don't know if he can unwrap it."

❖❖❖ "I like Christmas Eve best because that's when you get to pray to Santa Claus instead of God, and he really does something about it."

"What went on at your house this year for Christmas?" I asked five-year-old Regina.

"It was all mixed up. Santa put all the socks in the wrong places. And he forgot what I told him I wanted. Daddy said maybe he bumped his head coming down the chimney."

"Well, what did you ask Santa for that you didn't get?"

"I wanted a baby."

Eight-year-old Ben seemed to have an amazing memory for Christmas past: "When I was a baby, all anybody ever gave me for Christmas was clothes. They didn't know any better, and I couldn't talk to tell them."

Mary felt pretty good about her standing at Christmas time. "My mom knows Santa Claus in person," she told me. "She even knows his long-distance telephone number."

"That's great," I said. "So I'll bet you had a good Christmas."

"Yeah," Mary continued. "He always leaves more toys at our house than at any other house."

One child hadn't joined in at all with her first-grade classmates and their lively discussion of holidays. "Don't you like the holidays?" I asked.

"Not very much," she confessed. "We always work on the holidays because that's where all the money is."

Jeremy said he was never surprised at Christmas. "My mom has to take me shopping with her," he explained. "She sits me in a cart and blindfolds me so I can't see what she's buying. But I can hear toys."

Birthdays came in a clear second to Christmas, and most kids believed their birthdays were national holidays.

Grandma called ten-year-old Marc before school to wish him happy birthday.

"But Grandma," Marc protested, "I haven't been born yet. I wasn't born until 3:13 this afternoon."

Question: ***What do you like best about birthdays?***

❖❖❖ "Presents—all for me, none for my little sister."

❖❖❖ "Everybody has to be nice to me for a whole day, even when I'm spoiled. And nobody gets to watch the news."

❖❖❖ "Parties, and cake, and ice cream, and everything. That's a stupid question. Don't you have birthdays?"

❖❖❖ One little girl had a different answer: "I like age best."

"Age? What do you mean?"

"I like getting older. Pretty soon I'll be older than my mom. She's stopped having birthdays."

"My sister's the most spoiled kid in the whole world, and I hate her birthdays," complained Donny.

"Her birthday is on the Fourth of July, and she thinks all the fireworks and stuff are for her!"

"Easter," explained one kindergartner, "is the day we blow up balloons for God."

"Is that how you celebrate Easter?" I asked.

"Not just balloons," she continued. "Then we think about the cross—God's cross, that is—and then see who can find the most eggs. And that's Easter!"

"I like Easter," said Jenny, age eight, "because you get the beginning of nice weather and Jesus not being dead anymore."

Jenny's little sister Katy wasn't so sure she liked Easter. "I don't like the part about Jesus dying."

"He had to die," Jenny explained, "so we could go to heaven, Katy."

"Okay," said Katy reluctantly. "He can die, but I don't have to like it."

Four-year-old Laurie had a different perspective of Easter after a grueling hour coloring Easter eggs. She sighed, "Now I know how the Easter Bunny felt."

Question: When you trick-or-treat on Halloween, what's your best trick?

❖❖❖ "I keep changing costumes and going back to the same houses with the best candy."

❖❖❖ "I say, 'Trick or treat; smell my feet.' "

❖❖❖ "I dress up like a witch and meow at our cat."

❖❖❖ "My favorite day is Halloween because instead of all the big people scaring me, I get to scare big people!"

❖❖❖ "I'm always very tricky at Halloween," confided a nonthreatening-looking seven-year-old.

"What do you do on Halloween?" I asked cautiously.

And with a guilty grin, she confessed: "I trick my mom and dad and friends and give them candy when no one's looking."

❖❖❖ "My mom won't let me go trick or treating."

"Why not?"

"Because there's razor blades in all the apples, and poison in all the candy, and all the men in the neighborhood are waiting to jump out and capture you."

"So what do you do on Halloween night?" I asked.

"I stay home with my mom and lock all the doors and watch scary movies on TV."

One little girl didn't hesitate to let me know her favorite holiday.

"April Fools' Day!" she shouted.

"What's the best April Fools' joke you ever pulled?" I asked.

"Our whole family pulls this trick," she explained. "You see, we let our house get dirty all year. Then on April 1, we invite our friends to come over for a party. And when they come over, we shout, 'April Fools.' And the house is so dirty, they have to clean it up instead of have a real party."

One kindergarten boy felt July Fourth was the best holiday.

"Why do we celebrate the Fourth of July?" I asked.

"That's when fireworks were invented," he answered.

"Do we celebrate anything else on that day?"

He squinted and thought for a minute before bursting out with his answer: "Freedom!"

"Freedom from what?" I pressed.

"Freedom from school!"

"I hate Valentine's Day," Ralph told me in his second-grade classroom. "The teacher tells us we have to give valentines to everybody—even girls. Then they read the words already written on the valentines and act like it's you who wrote that stuff."

Five-year-old Michael made a valentine for his great-grandmother that read, "I love you, Grandma." Grandma was so proud of it that at dinner that evening she wanted Michael to tell the family what he had given her. "Tell them what the valentine you gave Grandma said," she urged.

Michael looked at his grandmother as if she had lost her mind. "It didn't say anything; it can't talk."

Most of the Thanksgiving scenes described by children are familiar and traditional.

Question: What's Thanksgiving like at your house?

❖❖❖ "We have a lot of food on a big table, and everybody just keeps passing it and passing it and passing it, so you hardly get to eat."

❖❖❖ "We celebrate with turkey and lots of relatives coming over and eating. But they don't bring presents until Christmas."

❖❖❖ "We say grace and chew with our mouths closed."

❖❖❖ "All the dads watch TV all day and night, and all the moms wash dishes."

There were exceptions to the traditional Thanksgiving celebrations.

❖❖❖ "We go around town and give food to everybody."

❖❖❖ "We give thanks for food and family . . . except for Tony."

"Why don't you give thanks for Tony?"

"Because he said he was going away to the service, but we all know better."

❖❖❖ "We cook chicken in the dark over a fire," said one eight-year-old.

"Why do you do that?"

"Mama says it's like a cookout, only inside. But I think it's because we don't have electricity."

❖❖❖ "On Thanksgiving we buy my mom flowers and turkey and cake and rings and necklaces and cookies."

❖❖❖ "On Thanksgiving we pray for God, instead of praying *to* God. We give him the day off."

Grown-ups make New Year's resolutions, but children can show determination too.

Question: What are you going to do differently this year?

❖❖❖ "This year," asserted a first-grade Missouri boy, "I'm going to be tougher with my sister!"

"How will you be tougher?" I asked.

"When she pushes me around, I'm not going to budge." Then he added, "This year, I'm going to be bigger."

❖❖❖ "I'm going to do trash."

"What do you mean?" I asked, puzzled.

"Do trash. When Mom says take out the trash, I'll *do* it."

❖❖❖ "I'm going to stay home from school and read books," volunteered a seven-year-old girl.

❖❖❖ "I'm going to quit college," said a first-grade student with thick-lensed glasses.

"Are you going to college now?" I asked.

"I was, but Dad says feeding cattle and doing chores is more important."

❖❖❖ "I'm going to ride bikes *outside*. You only get in trouble when you ride your bikes inside your house."

❖❖❖ "Mom says I'm going to go to the jungle or be nicer to my brother. . . . I think I'll go to the jungle."

Not many five-year-olds knew what Labor Day was. "What's Labor Day?" I asked.

No answers.

"Well, how do you celebrate Labor Day at your house?" I tried.

Finally Gavin answered. "We throw a big party and invite everybody to come in their underwear . . . NOT!"

Another good guess as to what Labor Day was all about came from a young man with eleven brothers and sisters.

"What do we celebrate on Labor Day?" I asked him.

"Mrs. Lincoln having a baby boy named Abraham."

Only seven-year-old Ryan had anything to say about Veterans Day. "Why is Veterans Day on the calendar?" he asked. "Is it the day dogs go to the veteran?"

✷ *CHAPTER 4* ✷

The Color of Money

Youth is the best time to be rich, and the best time to be poor.—Euripides, "Heracles"

At five-and-a-half, Berrigan was trying to teach her youngest sister, Hannah, fourteen months, about money. Berrigan held up a coin in front of Hannah and began: "This is a quarter. It's a single type of coin. No one puts it in her mouth."

The children I talked with seemed overall to have a better grasp of what money could buy than did kids a generation ago. No longer was a dollar considered a lot of money, enough to buy a car or a boat or a new house. Today's kids seldom made that error.

Question: What would you do if I gave you $5?

❖❖❖ "I'd save it so I could buy something when I got more."

❖❖❖ "I could get a guinea pig. But I couldn't get its cage or anything to go with it."

❖❖❖ "I could get a dog with it—if it was free."

❖❖❖ "A Nerf football."

❖❖❖ "A whoopee cushion."

❖❖❖ "Save it for college. Every little bit helps."

Some of the kids had other ideas:

❖❖❖ "Well, if I had a bad boyfriend, I could use it to buy me a good boyfriend, I think."

❖❖❖ "I'd give one-half to the Red Cross, one-half to the poor, and one-half to the people who live on the street."

"What would they do with it?" I asked.

"Buy a new box."

❖❖❖ "I'd buy me a lottery ticket and get me some real money!"

Question: What would you do if you won a million dollars in the lottery?

These were the most popular answers: "Buy new clothes!" "Go shopping at the mall!" "Buy candy!"

But some kids were much more specific as to what they'd purchase:

❖❖❖ "I'd buy the EPCOT Center."

❖❖❖ "Stocks and bonds."

❖❖❖ "Season tickets to all the games in the world!"

❖❖❖ "Horses."

❖❖❖ "A Porsche and a yacht."

❖❖❖ "I've already won a lot of money," Danny told me.

"You did?" I asked. "How much?"

"Thirteen dollars."

"How did you win it?"

"I won it playing my cousin in pool. I put five dollars in the bank and bought myself something with the rest."

"Well, what would you do if you won a million dollars?"

Without hesitation Danny answered, "I'd put it all in the bank, except keep forty dollars out."

"What would you do with the forty dollars?" I tried again.

"I'm not telling," he insisted. But I got the feeling he knew exactly what he'd do with it.

Ricky had to wait while his mother transacted business. The office was being remodeled, and one man was working on tearing up the wooden floor. After watching for a while Ricky felt sorry for him and asked, "What's the matter, Mister? Did you lose a dime?"

Question: *Who's the richest person in the world?*

❖❖❖ "The president!" (the person named most often)

❖❖❖ "Einstein."

❖❖❖ "People with big houses."

I was curious to know how kids saw themselves.

Question: *Is your family rich or poor?*

❖❖❖ "My family is rich," said Jon.

"How do you know?" I asked him.

"My parents have got a lot of money," he said, shaking his head slowly.

"But how do you know?" I repeated.

"Because they take it out and show it to me!"

❖❖❖ "My parents aren't rich," said one girl, "but my grandma is. She buys us lots and lots of presents, and she's still rich!"

❖❖❖ "Well," Katie began, "my parents are kind of richish and kind of poorish, right in between."

"How do you know?"

"Because we have really good clothes we wear to school and work. And we have really torn clothes we wear at home."

❖❖❖ "My parents are in the middle," Jimmy explained. "Our downstairs, where we have people sit when they come over to our house, is rich, with rich furniture and everything. But our upstairs, where we really live, is poor."

❖❖❖ "My parents aren't rich, and they aren't poor," one third-grade boy informed me. "They're middle."

"How do you know?" I asked.

"Rich people buy expensive things like mansions and Chevys. Poor people save for a couple of years for a bed. And if they ever get a house, they work on getting clothes a little bit at a time. Poor people only buy little toys, and rich people buy big toys. If you have both, then you're in the middle."

But many children felt their parents fell in the poor category.

❖❖❖ "My dad works at a steel factory making steel all day long. But we're poor because we spent all our money moving from Michigan to Ohio to Florida."

❖❖❖ "We just don't have much money, and that's why we're poor," said a kindergarten boy.

"Why don't you have much money?" I asked.

"Because we spent it all on going on airplanes and going to Florida and going to Sea World."

Alison, first grade, admitted that she had helped her mother tape a torn dollar bill back together. This led to my next question, "What happens to the old dollar bills when they get too worn-out to use any more?"

"You have to try to spend them as fast as you can," said Alison. "And if you can, you hide them in between new dollar bills when you pay for something."

Jenna had a different idea about old money. "Recycle it!"

Question: What's the most money you ever had?

❖❖❖ "Zero!" said Justin. "My brother has all the money in our family."

❖❖❖ "I have all the money in my family," Candice bragged.

"How much money do you have?" I asked.

"Whole bunches and bunches and more bunches!" she said.

"Where do you keep all this money?"

"In my penny bank at home."

❖❖❖ "I'm going to be the richest man in the world," said fourth-grade Michael.

"How are you going to manage that?"

"I'm going to be a state senator."

"I didn't know they made that much money," I said, puzzled.

"They don't. But you have a better chance of becoming president if you're a state senator for a while. And that's where the real money is."

I got a lot of different estimates when I asked first-graders to put a monetary value on themselves.

Question: How much money are you worth?

❖❖❖ "One million dollars."

❖❖❖ "One hundred dollars."

❖❖❖ "One hundred forty dollars."

❖❖❖ "Twelve thousand dollars."

❖❖❖ "Millions and millions," said one girl, shaking her head slowly.

❖❖❖ "Affinity!"

❖❖❖ "Now that depends on who we're selling to," Krista said softly. "As a slave, I wouldn't be worth too much because I'm so little—probably eleven dollars as a slave. But my mom would pay a whole lot of money for me."

When I asked the following question, I received every possible answer on the political spectrum—all from six- and seven-year-olds.

Question: Why are some people poor?

❖❖❖ "They don't want food because they're on a diet."

❖❖❖ "They spent their money on stuff that wasn't groceries. When you spend your money on groceries, they always give you money back."

❖❖❖ "They spent all their money."

❖❖❖ "They didn't invest it right."

❖❖❖ "The rich get all the tax breaks."

❖❖❖ "They lost their jobs and won't look for new ones."

❖❖❖ "The rich steal from the poor."

❖❖❖ "They dropped out of college and didn't finish high school."

❖❖❖ "They didn't spend their money wisely. They spent it on booze."

❖❖❖ "It's a drug problem."

❖❖❖ "Maybe their dad was an alcoholic."

❖❖❖ "They couldn't get their welfare check."

❖❖❖ "They didn't classify for the right job. So that left them with no job."

❖❖❖ "They're black."

❖❖❖ "Everything's too expensive."

❖❖❖ "Their parents were poor, and their grandparents were poor maybe."

❖❖❖ "They just are."

The subject of allowances brought up quite a few complaints.

"My mother is supposed to give me three dollars a week. And I'm supposed to sweep the floor and empty the dishwasher. But if I forget to sweep the floor, then I don't get my allowance. But she forgets to give me allowance all the time, and I still have to sweep the floor."

Question: How much do you get for an allowance, and what do you have to do to earn it?

From the kindergartners:

❖❖❖ "If I clean my room, . . . oh, I don't know. They never give me anything."

❖❖❖ "My parents don't give me any no matter what I do. But my grandma and grandpa give me money for nothing but love."

❖❖❖ "I used to get money, but not no more. Dad gots to save his money for a house next year."

And in a third-grade class:

❖❖❖ "My mom makes us a chart of chores: speech, spelling, clean room, other stuff. And we get one cent for each chore," one boy explained.

"What are you doing with all that money?" I asked.

"Saving for college. But I have another piggie bank, so don't worry about it."

❖❖❖ "I get one dollar for emptying the dishwasher and cleaning out the stinky rabbit cage."

❖❖❖ "Two bucks for playing with my hamster."

❖❖❖ "I get five dollars or three dollars for moving my books around from my bed to my backpack to the floor and around again."

❖❖❖ "I get five dollars for raking the yard and the kitchen and the oven."

❖❖❖ One fourth-grader made the loudest protest. "Seventy cents!" he complained, an air of disbelief about him. "Seventy measly cents! And I have to take out the garbage *and* bring it back in."

"Well," I began sympathetically, "how much do your friends get?"

"My cousin gets five dollars and he just takes out the garbage."

"Five dollars!"

"Now it's down to three fifty because of the way he talks to his parents."

All this talk of money led me in another direction.

Question: What things are free in life?

❖❖❖ "My mom sews for free."

❖❖❖ "Sometimes I clean our fireplace for free."

❖❖❖ "You can get free stuff at a free store sometimes, like baseball cards I don't care anything about."

❖❖❖ "I got a free hot dog at K mart."

❖❖❖ "Frozen yogurt in tiny cups at the mall. They're free because they want you to buy a bunch of it, but they can't make you."

❖❖❖ "Fifteen dollars' worth of quarters at Holiday Inn to play video games."

❖❖❖ "Where my dad works, you can sit on a bench for free—as long as you don't bother my dad."

❖❖❖ "Some money is free," Katie suggested. "I get it from my mom."

❖❖❖ "A twenty-dollar bill at Putt-Putt—I found one once."

❖❖❖ "At Grandma's, drinks are free!"

❖❖❖ "I get a free dollar every time I catch a rat in a trap. We have problems with rats. And if I get a rabbit, I get a dollar too."

❖❖❖ "Money you find in a sock by the baseball field, just on the other side of the woods—that's free, even if it's ten dollars."

❖❖❖ "Any pennies on the ground are free."

❖❖❖ "You can have free games with your friends."

❖❖❖ "Freedom is free."

❖❖❖❖❖❖

Question: Finish this sentence: Money can't buy ______________.

❖❖❖ ". . . blankets—if they're real expensive."

❖❖❖ ". . . wild animals in Africa."

❖❖❖ ". . . a new face."

❖❖❖ ". . . feet."

❖❖❖ ". . . inches."

"Money can't buy inches?" I queried, believing I'd heard wrong.

"Right. If you want to be taller, money can't help you."

❖❖❖ ". . . a good teacher."

❖❖❖ ". . . a real family."

❖❖❖ ". . . heaven."

❖❖❖ ". . . God."

✷ *CHAPTER 5* ✷

Rules and Resolutions

Most of us, by the time we're up
on the rules, are generally too old to play.
—Pappy Maverick, on "Maverick"

*V*ery few children knew how laws are made, but nearly everyone had an opinion on how laws are broken and what happens to people who break the law.

Question: What happens when you break laws?

❖❖❖ "Nothing," replied a midwestern kindergartner with a devilish grin. "Unless they catch you."

"You go straight to jail," Jenna answered. "Or you get shot."

"Or you have to sit in the corner," added Megan.

Jenna nodded agreement.

"I see." I went on: "And what could I do that was bad enough to send me to jail?"

"You could say a bad word," Megan said.

"Like what?" I asked.

But before Megan could answer, Jenna, sensing a trap, stuck her hand over her friend's mouth. "Don't tell her!" she said, giving me a suspicious glare.

❖❖❖ "When you break laws," said a seven-year-old, "you'll go to jail, where there's no food—only bread and water. And no bathrooms."

Question: What could I do to get thrown in jail?

❖❖❖ "Try to escape," offered William, a kindergartner.

"Or go through a red light," added classmate Greg.

"Nunh-uh," objected William.

"Yes," Greg said quietly. "If you go through a red light, you would go to jail."

"No sir!" William was almost shouting now, and both boys seemed to have forgotten about my interview with them. "Because my mom went through a red light yesterday. And she goes through red lights all the time, like every day. And she's not in jail. And she even speeds too."

Greg was not the slightest bit convinced. "Well, that's it."

"What?"

"She speeds. If you go through a red light slowly, you go to jail. But if you go through it speeding, they can't catch you. And they have to catch you before they throw you into jail."

❖❖❖ "You go to jail if you lie, cheat, steal, or kill somebody—unless they're bad people anyway," a curly-headed blonde girl informed me.

"So it's okay to kill somebody if he or she is bad?" I asked.

She thought, but only for a moment: "Well, it's okay to kill them if they kill you first."

❖❖❖ "If you get caught taking money out of a purse of somebody who isn't your mother, you go to jail," said a reflective first-grader.

"And if the purse belongs to your mother?" I ventured.

"Then you're in real trouble."

When I asked kindergartners and first-graders what New Year's resolutions they had made, we usually had to spend a little time defining terms.

Question: What's a resolution?

❖❖❖ The question drew blank stares until one little girl braved an answer: "Your parents have them . . . on New Year's . . . when they drink lots of champagne and beer."

❖❖❖ "It's when you wish you weren't so fat this year."

❖❖❖ "It's when everybody sets the clock forward and changes the last number on the name of the year."

❖❖❖ "It's the only day my uncle lets me smoke," said a first-grader.

Once everyone understood what resolutions were, most of the children discovered they already had them.

Question: What resolution did you make for the new year?

❖❖❖ "Clean my room." (the number one answer)

❖❖❖ "Exercise more."

❖❖❖ "Do the dishes."

❖❖❖ "Do education."

❖❖❖ "Eat horrible things on my plate without crying."

❖❖❖ "Feed my dog every two days."

"Why not every day?" I asked.

"It's *my* resolution!" he scolded.

❖❖❖ "I'm going to play with my pet more—a rabbit."

"How exactly do you play with a rabbit?" I asked.

"You take it out of the cage and move your finger like a toy and let him bite it."

❖❖❖ "I'll visit my granny every three days, and be nice to my brother one day a week," said a first-grade girl.

❖❖❖ "This year I'm not going to hit my brother so much. I'm going to yell at him more instead—unless he keeps smashing my head into the couch."

❖❖❖ When I asked for resolutions in one class, they had just finished making their New Year's resolutions. One little girl raised her hand, but before she could tell me her resolution, several of her classmates interrupted to tell me that the class had jointly made a resolution for her already. Then in unison they told me: "Don't talk so much about cats!"

When we talked about resolutions, I usually had to pull answers from the kids. But as soon as I asked for resolutions they'd like to make for someone else, hands waved all over the room.

Question: What resolutions would you make for your mom or dad?

❖❖❖ "Don't yell at your daughter!"

❖❖❖ "Clean your kids' rooms when they're at school."

❖❖❖ "Don't sleep so much."

❖❖❖ "Lose seventy pounds."

❖❖❖ "Give away your waterbed—to your son."

❖❖❖ "Stop having kids! My grandma has seventy-five grandchildren!"

❖❖❖ "Don't make me eat all that food. I get constipated!"

❖❖❖ "No more naps during the day."

❖❖❖ "Be my slave for a year."

❖❖❖ "Keep that workshop clean this year."

❖❖❖ "Be really nice to me—and really mean to my brothers."

❖❖❖ "I have one for my mom: Clean out the top of your dresser!"

❖❖❖ "I'd have my mom get a new name—Nicole. Yeah."

❖❖❖ "For one year when Daddy comes home, he could put his feet up."

❖❖❖ "Mom would curl her hair and wear different pants . . . and a different face."

❖❖❖❖❖❖

When Brittany told us her parents made a resolution that all the kids would have better table manners this year, she introduced a hot topic. Here are some of the table manners these six- and seven-year-olds relayed:

Table Manners

Say "please"—not "gimme that."
No bad words at the table (table cussing).
Never talk about food at the table.
No singing.
No snorting.
You can't talk about sick things like throwing up.
Don't chew on the table.
Don't cut the table with your knife when you're playing around.
Don't eat like a pig.
Don't eat your food in bed.
Never say "Do you like the potatoes?" or other food because you might make somebody lie.

Dad had his hands full keeping track of his two boys at the church supper. When they finished eating, both kids had a fair amount of grease and grime on face and hands. The oldest boy promptly wiped his face with his hand, and then turned to the nearest thing, the wall, and wiped his hands on the wall.

Deeply embarrassed, Dad yelled, "For crying out loud! Use your head, son!"

"No fair!" shouted the younger boy. "*I* had to use my napkin!"

On a family drive, six-year-old Mark downed his can of pop and announced that he had to use the restroom. His parents begged him to wait, to hang in there, but Mark just couldn't make it. As he looked at his pants and the wet seat, he said, "Now I know why they say don't drink and drive."

Question: Did you ever do something you'll never do again?

❖❖❖ "Dive in the shallow end."

❖❖❖ "Play football," said a six-year-old boy.

"Why won't you play football again?" I asked.

"Because my brother always runs at me whenever I get the ball, and he won't let me run with it. And when he gets the ball, he runs the other way so I can't catch him. And sometimes he kicks it really far and jumps up and down and yells. And sometimes, when I have the ball and run, he jumps on top of me."

Football. I had to agree, it didn't sound like much fun.

❖❖❖ "Take a running start down the hall, into the bathroom, try to stand on my hands on the side of the bathtub, and have no water in the tub."

❖❖❖ "Talk my little brother into chopping down our cherry tree."

❖❖❖ "I'll never climb onto the roof and jump off again. They might find me out."

❖❖❖ "I'll never pinch nobody again!"

"Why not?"

"Because my dad kicked me all the way up the stairs!"

❖❖❖ "I'll never jump out of my top bunk onto the bean bag chair and miss again."

❖❖❖ "I'll never jump out of the window again! I was just lucky that my brother caught me this time."

❖❖❖ "I'll never try to hit a dog again."

"Why did you hit the dog in the first place?" I asked.

"Because he bited my foot, that's why."

"Why did he bite your foot?" I asked.

"Because I kicked him."

Animals played quite a role in the never-again vows.

❖❖❖ "Never again will I dress our cat in people clothes. She scratched my heart out!"

❖❖❖ "I won't run away from dogs, because when you do, they run right over the top of you."

❖❖❖ And my favorite animal resolution: "Never pat a beehive."

Question: Are there any unreasonable rules at your house?

❖❖❖ "We can't go outside in the winter!" said a kindergartner wearing a #19 football jersey and a scowl.

"You can't go outside—at all?" I challenged.

"Not unless you have boots on and a coat."

"Well, that sounds pretty sensible to me," I had to admit.

"No, it's insane," he insisted. "No boots, no fresh air. Kids need fresh air."

❖❖❖ "My mom makes us go to bed earlier in the summer than in the winter—while it's still light outside!"

❖❖❖ "I have to do all my homework at home!"

❖❖❖ Eric talked as if he had just completed his tiring round of chores. "I'm an only child," he complained, "so I have to feed the dogs, do all the dishes, sweep the walks, gather the eggs, and clean up after my sisters!"

"Wait a minute," I said. "Clean up after your sisters? I thought you said you were an only child."

"I'm the only child who works!"

❖❖❖ "Only two cookies a day!" said a pleasingly plump second-grader.

❖❖❖ "No glue on your own body."

❖❖❖ "Bed at 10:30 or 11:50 on school nights," complained one kindergartner.

❖❖❖ "No couch-flipping."

❖❖❖ "No going down the stairs head-first, and no axe-play in the garage. That's it."

❖❖❖ "Don't yell in the bathroom when your dad has third shift."

❖❖❖ "Never throw rocks at beehives."

❖❖❖ "Don't flush pennies down the toilet, even if they're yours."

❖❖❖ "Don't drink out of the bathroom glass unless you're sick."

❖❖❖ "Don't fight when Grandpa and Grandma are over. And act like you like them."

❖❖❖ "Don't back-talk, or you get a bloody lip at my house," said one second-grade girl.

"What kind of punishment could the rest of you expect for breaking these rules?" I asked her class.

"A whippin'," said one.

"If you bark like a dog at our house," complained her friend, "my dad will pull down your underwear and spank you with a wooden stick—but only for barking like a dog."

One little guy sighed, leaned back in his chair, and said, "Man, all I have to do is sit in a chair for a couple of minutes no matter what I do. You should come to my house."

Question: Are there any silly rules you found waiting for you when you started school?

❖❖❖ "We can't wear shorts!" said a kindergartner in a fashionable dress with matching socks and hair ribbon.

"We can too!" said the girl next to her, sporting blue jeans and a sweatshirt.

"Well, we can't when it's winter."

❖❖❖ "They only give you fifteen minutes for lunch here," said an incredulous five-year-old.

"And only one minute for breakfast!" said his buddy. "But I guess that's more at home."

❖❖❖ "Don't run in the classroom," said another.

❖❖❖ "You can't get up when the teacher's reading, even if you have to go to the bathroom really bad."

"And he *does* have to go really bad!" testified his friend.

He nodded. "And, you have to ask permission to get a lousy Kleenex!"

❖❖❖ "Don't back-talk your teacher when she tells you you can't slide on the ice. And you can't eat snow or snowballs."

"Where do all these rules come from?" I asked one second-grade class.

One young man in the back of the room raised his hand. "My parents get them from my grandma's house."

Question: What can't you do that others can *do?*

❖❖❖ "We're not allowed to play with dolls," said a seven-year-old girl.

"Ever?" I asked.

"Never—if they're still in the store on shelves."

◆◆◆ "I can't talk to strangers," said an angry seven-year-old.

"And you think other children can talk to strangers?" I quizzed.

"Other children know them, and they're not strangers."

◆◆◆ "I can't kick my brother."

◆◆◆ "We can't point guns at each other."

◆◆◆ "I'm not supposed to tell ghost stories after midnight."

◆◆◆ "When my cousin invites girls over and shows off for them, Mom won't let me show off."

◆◆◆ "No snowballs or arrows at the dog."

◆◆◆ "No ice down Dad's pants."

◆◆◆ "I can't eat swimming pool water."

◆◆◆ "Don't be sneaky."

Question: What's the Golden Rule?

◆◆◆ "It's Jesus, I think."

◆◆◆ "Don't have abortions."

◆◆◆ "It's what heaven is made of at the gate."

◆◆◆ "The Golden Rule is: Get diamonds."

❖❖❖ "You can always buy lots of treasures if you have enough money."

❖❖❖ "Don't be bad in class."

❖❖❖ "It's the biggest, most daring rule. You have to try really hard to do it. It's that you gotta do what teacher says and follow directions."

❖❖❖ "Listen, and if people get hurt, be quiet so you can hear them crying."

❖❖❖ "The Golden Rule is: Clean your room."

Alicia tried hard to be good and mind her aunt while her mother stayed with her brother in the hospital for a week. On the last day of her visit, her aunt told Alicia that tomorrow she would get to go home.

"Well, just one more day to be good," was her response.

A couple of fifth-grade boys were horsing around in their Catholic schoolroom when, to their amazement, the teacher spied them out of the corner of her eye.

She duly reprimanded them, then overheard the following conversation:

"How did she see us?" one boy asked.

Wayne replied, "You forgot. She has good parochial vision!"

✸ *CHAPTER 6* ✸

It's a Hard-Knocks Life

When you are eight years old, nothing is any of your business.—Lenny Bruce

Most kids are quick to tell us that being a kid isn't as easy as we might think. Grown-ups take up so much of their time that kids never seem to have enough time to do what they like best.

Question: What do you like to do best?

❖❖❖ "Walk around the block—both ways."

❖❖❖ "Ride my bike and read."

❖❖❖ "Supersoak the house."

❖❖❖ "Homework," said a second-grade girl.

When all her classmates booed, I asked her why she liked to do homework so much.

"It's more fun than schoolwork!" she said.

Most children seemed to be under the impression that their parents get mad at them a lot.

Question: What makes your parents angry?

❖❖❖ "Not coming home by dark."

❖❖❖ "Yelling, 'Daddy's home!' when he's not."

❖❖❖ "When you ignore them."

❖❖❖ "Eating crayons."

"Why do you eat crayons?" I asked the five-year-old girl before me.

She smiled slightly. "To make them angry."

❖❖❖ "Talking to strangers anytime or to Mom before five A.M."

❖❖❖ "Hanging up my nephew on a fence."

❖❖❖ "Pulling my little brother's pants down and sitting him up a tree."

❖❖❖ "Putting toothpaste in my ears. When it dries, I can't hear them screaming at me."

❖❖❖ "Walking in my socks. It makes Mom cuss."

❖❖❖ "Spitting at the table."

❖❖❖ "Commercials."

❖❖❖ "People dying."

❖❖❖ "My mother hates it when she's talking on the phone and me and my sister wrestle," Katy told me.

"What does she do?" I asked.

"She keeps talking all nice and sweet on the telephone, but she makes supermean faces at us and shakes her fist at us."

"Does that make you stop wrestling?"

"No."

"Why not?"

"Because it's the best time. All she can do is look mean. And we can always go outside before she finishes talking on the phone."

❖❖❖ "My parents hate it when I talk back," said a mature second-grade girl.

"What exactly is talking back?" I asked.

"I say the same stuff back to them that they always say to me."

❖❖❖ Cicely's answer surprised me. "Mom gets mad at me when my brother gets angry at her. He kicks her when he gets real angry at her."

"I don't quite understand," I confessed. "Your mother gets angry with you when your brother kicks her?"

"Yes. I laugh."

❖❖❖ "My father, he always gets mad at me and my brothers when we go to the Laundromat," first-grader Lee said.

"Why is that?"

"There's just too much mischief to get into in your average Laundromat."

❖❖❖ "My uncle always yells at me for nothing," complained a third-grade student.

"Give me an example of something he yelled at you for," I asked.

"Like being in his workshop."

"You mean he doesn't like you to go into his workshop?"

"Mostly he doesn't like me playing with his blowtorch."

❖❖❖ One little boy complained, "My dad sneaks me out of the house when it snows and plays in the snow with me. Then we come in all wet and cold, and he blames it on me. And Mom gets mad at me!"

❖❖❖ "Acting like I don't hear them say 'Turn off the TV!' "

❖❖❖ "Biting Daddy."

❖❖❖ "When somebody climbs to the third shelf of Daddy's bookcase and knocks off all the books. That'll do it."

❖❖❖ "When I hit my sister with a bike."

❖❖❖ "My parents always get mad at me and my brother and my sister whenever we drive in a car anywhere."

❖❖❖ "If you want to make my mom mad, you say, 'Daddy lets me do it.' "

❖❖❖ One brother and sister team had trouble narrowing the field.

"Well," began the brother, "I think it's when we have manure fights."

His sister didn't agree with him right away. "No," she said at last, "I think they get madder when I get in the car and lock all the doors and won't let them in. Especially when they're in a hurry."

Question: How do your parents punish you when you do something really bad?

❖❖❖ "Make me clean my room. And if I'm really bad, they make me clean under my bed."

❖❖❖ "They send me to my room, unless I just hit my sister. They don't care if I hit my sister."

❖❖❖ "If it's something horrible, like breaking the TV, they ground me for a whole day!"

❖❖❖ "My parents take all my toys away and give them to my little brother."

❖❖❖ "They let my brother play with my remote-control auto until he breaks it."

❖❖❖ "They make me walk the cat at night."

❖❖❖ "If I do something really bad, like putting make-up on my little brother and curling his hair, and putting a dress on him to make him into a little sister, they get really mad. And they say, 'No "Different Strokes" on TV for two weeks!' "

❖❖❖ "My parents make me go to bed at 5:20 Central Standard Time. How would you like that?"

❖❖❖ "If I do something bad, I can do it again if I say I'm sorry. But if I do the same thing three times, I'll have to stay in my room until suppertime."

Question: What's the worst punishment?

❖❖❖ "My mother hit me for punching my brother," complained an eight-year-old boy.

"So," I said, "you punched your brother, and your mother punched you?"

"Yeah," he said. "I just hate baby boys!"

❖❖❖ "The worst punishment is when you didn't do anything," Maritta, age eight, told me. "My mother always believes other people's kids before she believes me. I don't know why. She believes my brothers before she believes me. They told her that I pulled a knife on them, and I got a whipping. I didn't pull no knife on them. That's the worst punishment."

❖❖❖ "My mama says that if you take drugs, you punish yourself. You make yourself ugly and skinny. And then you make yourself into a skeleton and die."

❖❖❖ Kids sometimes get into contests to determine who gets the worst punishment for the least crime.

"I only hit my sister, and I had to stay inside all day," Kevin complained.

"When I jump on my bed, my mom makes me go to the store all by myself," said Julie.

"I yell through the house and I get grounded for two months," Cary said.

But Tommy won with this story. "I acted up the day before my birthday. And then on my birthday everybody sang, 'Happy Birthday—No presents. Happy Birthday—No presents. Happy Birthday to Tommy. Happy Birthday—No presents.' "

Question: What's the hardest part about being a kid?

❖❖❖ "Parents!"

❖❖❖ "All the maybes."

❖❖❖ "They let us eat candy and we get constipated," said one second-grader.

"Do your parents really let you eat candy whenever you want?" I asked.

"Well, they have it in the house all the time. Same thing."

❖❖❖ "The hardest part," said a soft-looking, shy first-grade girl, "is that I'd rather be a black cat or a bull."

❖❖❖ Laura complained, "The hardest part is making your bed, because it shakes. I have a waterbed."

❖❖❖ "You can't go over to anybody's house without permission, and when you cuss, you get a whippin'! I can't wait till I grow up."

❖❖❖ "The hardest part is writing and spelling. The rest is okay."

❖❖❖ "Men teachers."

❖❖❖ "Spending the best part of a week in school."

❖❖❖ "Going to bed each and every single night."

❖❖❖ "Not fighting with brothers and sisters."

❖❖❖ "Being sad all the time," said another quiet first-grader.

"What makes you sad all the time?" I asked.

"People dying. My grandfather died, and then somebody else I can't tell you about or I'll get a whippin'."

❖❖❖ "Keeping pets alive is the hardest. First my turtle ran away. Then I had a fish, but somebody ate it. And then I had a cat, but somebody ran over it. My mother called 911 when my cat got ran over, but it didn't help."

❖❖❖ "The worst part about being a kid," said a fragile-looking Melissa, "is that you have to follow directions from everybody. And lots of times they all give different directions."

❖❖❖ "The hardest part about being a kid," Tyler said matter-of-factly, "is that you're the one who has to walk the snake and pick up the cat mess."

❖❖❖ "The best part about being a kid," said Alicia, "is when I hit my brother in the stomach and he goes 'ooomph!' The worst part about being a kid is when my parents see me hit my brother in the stomach and I get no TV for a year!"

❖❖❖ "The toughest part about growing up," Cody confided, "is that your brothers are still littler than you are and you have to be the responsible one no matter how old they get!"

❖❖❖ "I have no girlfriend," seven-year-old Steven said sadly. "And that's the toughest part."

Jen disagreed. "No, the hardest part is having your parents and stepparents fight over you. They need to act like they're grown-ups."

❖❖❖ "Well, sometimes," began a third-grade girl, "you get all excited about getting presents at Christmas. And then you don't get anything good."

"So," I suggested, "tell me what the worst present you ever got was."

"A rubber band on a book," she said shyly.

"Anybody else?" I challenged.

"Grandma—but you can't tell her because it would hurt her feelings—got me a cheap dolly and the arms and legs fell off."

"I got Care Bear sheets! And I'm nine years old!"

"And I got a Superman pajamas!" said a humiliated fellow.

Other Worst Gifts

Clothes

Weird puzzles of Rochester, New York

Ohio State football helmet—when you live in Michigan.

Toothbrush
A huge teacher's math book, with no answers
Rotten cheese
A sack of coal
A bike you can't ride because you're too little
Anything that comes in your stocking
Lip gloss
An orange
A calendar where you learn a new word a day
Golf balls all chopped up
Newspapers

❖❖❖❖❖❖

Five-year-old Ryan tried to help his mother dress his three-month-old sister, Hannah. But no matter how hard he tried, he couldn't get her sleeper unsnapped. Finally, out of frustration, he declared, "These must be childproof."

Finally, I had to turn the tables on the kids.

Question: Is there anything tough about being a parent?

❖❖❖ "You have to wait on your child night and day, hand and foot!"

❖❖❖ "Diapers!"

❖❖❖ "Bills!"

❖❖❖ "Punishing your children—if you love them."

❖❖❖ "Kids screaming all over the house."

❖❖❖ "Headaches."

❖❖❖ "Taking kids to the bathroom everywhere—even in the middle of the night."

Question: Since life is so hard, have you ever tried to run away?

❖❖❖ "I ran away," said Jenna, age six, "because my mommy was not being very nice to me. I got all ready to make a break when I could, but I didn't go."

"Why didn't you go through with it?" I asked.

"Because my mommy would miss me too much."

❖❖❖ Jeffry had a similar experience. "I fought with my daddy and hit him. Then I had to run away because he made me cry."

"But you came back?"

"Yes. I missed him."

❖❖❖ "I did it!" Craig said proudly. "I ran away from my family, where even my brother couldn't get me. And they couldn't find me and I fell asleep, and they went crazy!"

"Where were you holed up?" I asked.

"Right under the couch."

❖❖❖ Jesse, age seven, said sure, he had run away. "I went about ten miles down the road. And then I came ten miles back."

"That was quite a trip," I said.

"And I did this five times."

❖❖❖ "I ran away to the hospital," Kyle said, "because my brother was beating me."

"You mean you had to go to the hospital because your brother hurt you?"

"No! I went there because it's quiet there. I just curled up on the picnic table and went to sleep."

❖❖❖ "I tried to run away, but I got nabbed taking cookies from the kitchen. They didn't care if I went, but I couldn't take the cookies."

❖❖❖ "My parents got mad at me and told me to go to my room. So I went, but I climbed out the window. Our street dead-ends into a graveyard. I hung around there for a while, but I got scared and came home."

❖❖❖ One little girl began, "I ran away because my mom got mad at me because I kicked my brother."

"Why did you kick your brother?"

"He wouldn't run away with me."

"Well, where did you go?"

"I went to my girlfriend's house. Pretty soon my mom came over looking for me, but I hid, and my girlfriend said, 'No, your daughter's not here.' Then my mom said she was tired from looking and could she please come in and get a drink of water. So my friend let her in, but it was a trick. She grabbed me and took me home."

❖❖❖ Craig sat and listened to several stories of running away. Finally he said, "I wanted to run away, but Mom and Dad say I can't."

✸ *CHAPTER* 7 ✸

The Best of Times and the Worst of Times

Children are tyrants. They contradict their parents, gobble their food, and tyrannize their teachers.
—Socrates (470–399 B.C.)

Question: Describe the best day of your life.

❖❖❖ "My best day," said Leo, a heavyset second-grader who had to sit in a special desk by the teacher so he wouldn't disrupt the other students, "was one day last year when we stayed in from recess and drew pictures. The teacher liked mine. She hung it up."

❖❖❖ "Today is my best day," said Heidi. "Every day today is my best day."

❖❖❖ "The day I took Jesus as my Savior at bedtime," said Mark.

❖❖❖ Jon surprised us all by telling us where he spent his favorite day. "My favorite day was when I saw the dentist in Cleveland." Seeing that we all disagreed with his choice of best, Jon went on, "He had fun fixing my teeth, and he put in an expander."

❖❖❖ Nathan described his best day: "Virginia Beach! We found neat animals on the shore, half buried, with pieces of body here and pieces of legs over there."

❖❖❖ Meredith said her best time was also her worst time. "I'll give you the worst first," she told me. "I climbed a tree by an old country school and jumped off and busted my arm."

"And that was also your best day?" I asked.

"Yes, because my friend was there and she gave me her own drink from her own lunch."

Question: Describe the worst day of your life.

❖❖❖ "The day my sister was born."

❖❖❖ "I got in trouble for knocking over the teacher's water onto her desk and papers."

"Well, that sounds like an accident," I offered.

"I knocked it over with a soccer ball."

❖❖❖ "My worst day," said Aaron, still in kindergarten, "was when I shot my brother with a BB gun."

"That sounds like your brother's worst day, Aaron," said one of his classmates.

"But I forgot to tell you, he hit me over the head with a baseball bat first!"

❖❖❖ "I'll tell you when my worst day was," said a quiet kindergartner. "My mom got so mad at my dad, she turned off TV. Then Dad got so mad, he smashed the can on the table and threw the channel changer on the floor. Then he left for two hours. I thought he wasn't ever coming back."

❖❖❖ "My worst day," Miranda explained, "was when I went fishing."

"Didn't you catch any fish, Miranda?" I asked.

"Yeah. I caught one, but he pulled *me* in!"

❖❖❖ Amy didn't have to think twice when I asked what her worst day was. Two words: "Root canal."

Injuries and illnesses made up many worst days for fourth-graders.

❖❖❖ "I was sick all over Disney World," said Bethany.

❖❖❖ Michael complained he had a fever on vacation and had to stay in the hotel room all day.

"Where was that?" I queried.

"Some big hotel somewhere."

❖❖❖ Adam claimed his worst day came when he knocked his chin open on the church. And Lonnie had a similar tale to tell. "I split my head open," he told us.

"How did you manage that?" I asked him.

"Playing milk with my cousin."

❖❖❖ "I dived from the toilet seat into the tub," Drew said in a raspy voice.

"What happened? Did you miss?"

"No, I hit it. Only the problem was, there was nothing in the tub except a broken squirt gun . . . and then me."

❖❖❖ John's pain, however, was of a different kind. "The worst days are when I get Fs on tests. And the other worst days are when I invite kids over to play, but they don't come."

Question: What's the worst thing you ever did?

❖❖❖ "I threw a brick through our window," a six-year-old girl admitted.

"Why?" I asked, surprised. "Was it an accident?"

"No," she replied quietly. "This brick was lying around inside our house, and I thought it needed to be outside."

"That's nothing," said her male classmate, not about to be outdone. "I threw my brother through our window!"

❖❖❖ "I used to write bad notes about my brother and mail them to the principal."

❖❖❖ "I scared my sister," Emily told us.

"Oh, I do that all the time," said her friend. "I hide behind her door and jump out and scare her when she comes in."

"Is that what you do?" I asked Emily.

"No," said Emily. "I tell her I'm going to kill her."

❖❖❖ One eight-year-old girl admitted her worst action. "I kissed a boy."

"What happened to you?" I asked.

"I had to stay in my room every night and no TV. And I was only seven."

"Was that the end of it?"

"I kissed again when I was eight, but nobody knew about it." She thought a minute and added, just for the record, "I also kissed a boy when I was six, but I was too little to know what we were doing."

❖❖❖ "The worst thing I ever did was decorating," Stuart told me, a gleam in his eye.

"That doesn't sound too bad," I commented.

"With chocolate syrup," he finished.

❖❖❖ "The worst thing I ever did?" Shandi repeated. "A hundred push-ups. I was sore for a week!"

❖❖❖ "I shot a frog," said one fourth-grader.

"How many times?" his buddy asked.

"Once. Did you ever shoot a frog?"

"Sure. Fourteen times," he answered proudly, "and then we hung him from our front porch!"

❖❖❖ "I started the car and pushed the gas pedal," Andrew admitted. "And that was before I had my passport."

Question: What's the best thing that ever happened to you?

❖❖❖ "I swam in the deep part."

❖❖❖ "The best thing is that I can play on earth without falling off."

❖❖❖ "I won't tell you the best thing that ever happened to me, but it has something to do with food."

❖❖❖ "Guilt. It makes Mom and Dad take me to parks, to the circus, to the movie, and everywhere. They feel real guilty if they don't."

❖❖❖ Dan, dressed in crisp, black pants and a button-down shirt, didn't hesitate with his answer: "The greatest thing that ever happened to me was becoming a cowboy."

❖❖❖ "May 23rd." (Guess when her birthday is.)

❖❖❖ One little girl asked if she could tell the best thing *she* ever did.

"We sent God our yellow kitten Pokey. Pokey died."

Question: What's the best thing, and what's the worst thing, about you?

❖❖❖ Aaron was only in kindergarten, but he was ready with his answer almost instantly. "The best thing about me is that I know karate and I love my mom. The worst thing about me is that I broke my leg doing kicking karate on another kid."

❖❖❖ Natalie couldn't wait to share her best and worst. "The best part about me is that when Katie bugs me, I don't bug her back and I don't tattle. The worst thing is that nobody ever believes me when I tell them Katie is bugging me!"

❖❖❖ "The worst thing about me," said Bobby, "is that I'm fat. But the best thing about me is I'm a good swimmer and I can float."

❖❖❖ "I guess," Quentin said deliberately, "the worst thing about me is that I'm clumsy. I'm so clumsy that when my mom hits me, I fall down!"

❖❖❖ "The best thing about me," Chris said, "is that I love the rain and the mud and all the mud puddles. And the worst thing is I like to push kids in mud puddles."

❖❖❖ "I know what the worst thing about me is," said Dan. "I pick my nose. But I'm good at sports."

If kids were quick to spot their own bests and worsts, they were even quicker to identify parental weak spots.

Question: ***What's the worst thing about your parents?***

❖❖❖ "The worst thing my mom ever did," reported one first-grade girl, "was grounding me for biting my friend's rear end."

"Why did you bite your friend's rear end?" I asked.

"It was an accident! I was hungry, and I didn't notice it was her rear end. And my mom wouldn't believe me."

❖❖❖ "The worst thing my parents do," reported Jeremiah, "is soccer."

I tried to understand. "You mean you all play soccer together?"

"No," he answered. "I play soccer. They sit there and yell at me."

"You should be happy," Kelly told him. "The worst thing my parents do is they don't come to any of my games."

❖❖❖ "The worst thing about my parents," said a lively kindergartner named Scott, "is that they're bigger than I am!"

❖❖❖ "The worst thing about my parents," said Lorry, "is that they spoil me. I like that."

❖❖❖ "The best thing about my parents," Tyler said, "is that they had me. The worst thing they did was to have my brother."

❖❖❖ The most frequent answer I received to the question about the worst thing parents do was "Fight."

"I hate it when they yell at each other!" said one kindergartner.

"Yeah," agreed her classmate. "They argue until one of them gets up and leaves."

"What do parents argue about?" I asked.

"Me," said one girl.

"Money," said a boy in her class.

"Stupid stuff," said a second girl, "like taking the wrong road when we're driving in the car, or being late to meetings, or where to shop. They make me crazy."

Most kids have an idea about what they'd like to be when they grow up, what they'd consider the best job to have. They usually have an opinion about what the worst job would be, too.

Question: What would be the worst job you could have?

❖❖❖ "Toilet-cleaner-outer in a town where nobody ever flushes."

❖❖❖ "Chores."

❖❖❖ "I don't want to be a nurse," Brittany told me emphatically.

"Why not?"

"Because I *do* want to own horses and a piano."

"And you couldn't do that if you were a nurse?"

"No," she assured me. "Then you'd have to be a piano teacher."

❖❖❖ Heather wasn't sure what she wanted to be when she grew up, but she was certain about what she didn't want to be. "I don't want to work in a chemical store!"

"Why not?"

"Because chemicals have things in them that can hurt you, so you have to wash your hands all day long. And they can still hurt you."

❖❖❖ "I wouldn't want to be a soccer player," Megan said.

Aaron interrupted. "You couldn't be a soccer player anyway because you're a girl!"

"I could too!"

"Could not"

"If I want to be a soccer player, Aaron, I'll be a soccer player!"

"You said you'd never want to be a soccer player," Aaron said.

"Well," Megan assured him. "I do."

❖❖❖ "The worst job you could have is a waiter."

"And what would your best job be?" I asked.

"A cook."

"I don't want to be a cook," said her fellow first-grader, Maria.

"Why don't you want to be a cook?" I asked Maria.

"Because I hate salt, and you have to use it when you're a cook."

❖❖❖ "I want any job where I can sit back and relax," said a laid-back third-grader. "Like computer people or scientists. The worst job is anything outside where you have to move around all the time."

❖❖❖ Matt, a handsome kindergartner, scooched his chair as close as possible to mine, looked up at me with big, brown eyes, and told me what his favorite job would be: "An author. I want to write children's books."

"That's great!" I said. "Just like I do. What would be your worst job?"

"Oh, baby-sitting or something like that. I hate children."

❖❖❖ One first-grade boy seemed to know what he wanted from life, but I never did quite grasp the logic. "I want to be an airplane fixer and a computer scientist," he told me. "And I don't ever want to be a kid's lunchbox."

A surprising number of children said their worst job would be doctor. So although many kids named doctor as their best job, being a doctor also got the second-most votes for the worst job, right behind being a garbage collector.

❖❖❖ "I don't want to be a doctor," said Julie.

"Why is that?"

"Because you might be delivering a baby and they would make you kill the baby because it had something wrong with it and the mommy and daddy didn't want it. And I couldn't do that."

❖❖❖ "I couldn't stand touching all that old blood," said one girl with a shiver.

"What do you want to be?" I asked.
"A waiter."

❖❖❖ "I don't want to be a doctor," Adam said, "because you have to cut people open. But I also don't want to be a taxi driver in a big city."

Beauty is in the eye of the beholder, especially if that beholder is a child.

Question: Tell me the prettiest and the ugliest thing you've ever seen.

❖❖❖ "The prettiest thing is a walking horse, and the ugliest thing is anyone who tries to scare me."

❖❖❖ "The prettiest thing is you," Megan said, knowing that answer would get her into my book.
"How nice of you, Megan," I said.
"I thought it was you when you were talking to us during the assembly in the gym. You looked beautiful, but I was on the back row. I'm not sure now."

❖❖❖ "The ugliest thing," Sasha told me, "is boys. I like pigs and hogs better than boys."

❖❖❖ "The prettiest is my grandma and grandpa. The ugliest is my warts. I have millions of them."
"How did you get those warts?" I asked.
"Frogs doing their business on my hands."

❖❖❖ "The prettiest thing is a dandelion that falls apart when you blow on it."

❖❖❖ "The ugliest thing I ever saw is Texas."

❖❖❖ "An eyeball—that's the ugliest. Did you ever get a good look at an eyeball?"

❖❖❖ "The prettiest—the Nutcracker dance of the Plum Fairies; and the ugliest—my drawings of the ballerinas."

❖❖❖ "Blue flowers are the prettiest, and broccoli is the ugliest. That was easy."

❖❖❖ "I saw a picture of heaven, and it was the prettiest. Spinach is the ugliest."

❖❖❖ "Christmas is prettiest, and snakes are ugliest."

If beauty is in the eye of the beholder, so is humor.

Question: What's the funniest thing you ever saw?

❖❖❖ "People crossing their eyes on purpose."

❖❖❖ "Clowns!"

❖❖❖ "My mom."

❖❖❖ "My cousin's face."

❖❖❖ "Fish eating with their mouths open."

❖❖❖ "Steven, when he fell in the toilet."

❖❖❖ "Jon's dog asleep."

❖❖❖ "My sister getting dressed. She's fourteen and worries about everything!"

❖❖❖ "My dad when I put double-sided tape on the toilet seat."

❖❖❖ "The funniest thing I ever saw? The adult swim at the pool."

✸ *CHAPTER 8* ✸

Growing Up and Growing Old

I like life. It's something to do.—Ronnie Shakes

Ask any child between the ages of four and six what he or she would like to be when grown-up. Chances are, the answer will surprise you.

Question: What do you want to be when you grow up?

❖❖❖ "I want to be a fire engine!" Shawn announced.

"You mean a fireman, don't you?" I corrected.

"No. I mean a fire engine. Jimmie's going to be a fireman." And Jimmie nodded in concurrence.

❖❖❖ "I want to be a ninja disguised as a violinist."

❖❖❖ "When I'm eight, I want to be a teaching teacher. And when I'm twelve, I want to be a dancing teacher."

❖❖❖ "I want to be a football player and knock everybody's air out."

❖❖❖ "I want to be a cleaning lady when I grow up," announced a delicate gal in a pretty white dress. "I just love to scrub."

❖❖❖ "I want to be an angel when I grow up," Anita told me.

"What's an angel do?"

"Angels take care of old people and dentists. And they take bad people to hell."

❖❖❖ "I want to be in the FBI."

"What's that?"

"Don't you know?" he asked me.

"Not really," I confessed.

"I'm not really sure," he admitted. "Maybe I'll be a woodworker or a jet fighter pilot instead. Everybody knows what they do."

❖❖❖ "I want to be a professional," said Elizabeth.

"What's a professional do?"

"A professional is on committees and comes home late every night and never gets dirty until she gets home."

❖❖❖ "I'm going to be a nurse, a swim teacher, a doctor, and an airplane teacher."

❖❖❖ "I'm going to be a teacher," said Dawn.

"What's the hardest part about being a teacher?" I asked.

"Worrying."

"What would you do with a kindergartner who was really acting up?"

"Tell him to stop it."

"What if he wouldn't stop?"

"I'd give him time-out to sit in the corner or go to the principal's office."

"And if he still wouldn't stop acting up?"

"I'd marry him. That would keep him real quiet."

My trips to inner-city schools in Cleveland, Chicago, and Los Angeles rewarded me with many of the best interviews. When I asked these children what they wanted to be when they grew up, they revealed their dreams.

❖❖❖ "I want to be a movie star and dance and sing," Marissa said.

"Why do you want to be a movie star?"

"So I can wear fancy clothes, live in a fancy house, and be famous."

❖❖❖ "I want to be Cinderella when I grow up," confided Dominique, age seven, "and marry a king."

❖❖❖ "I may be Batman when I grow up," George said.

"Why Batman?"

"I was Dracula for Halloween."

We stared at each other a minute in silence. Then he explained, "I just dressed up as Dracula for Halloween. Dracula probably dressed up as me for Halloween. If I'm Batman when I grow up, I can still dress up as me every Halloween."

❖❖❖ "I want to be a lawyer," said Earl, a third-grader. "Then I can sue everybody and take all their money."

❖❖❖ Many students reported their plans to become doctors. The reason given most often? Doctors are rich. But Angeline, who was in the second grade, said she wanted to help people. So I pressed further:

"Angeline, what's the hardest part about being a doctor?"

"When people die—bringing them back to life. Now that's hard!"

"What would you do if I came to you and you discovered I had a horrible disease and was going to die?"

Angeline touched my arm in superb bedside manner and said softly, "I'm really sorry you're going to die now."

Not everyone in the inner city wanted to be a doctor or a lawyer. Listen to the diversity of answers from kindergartners through third-graders.

❖❖❖ Willie told me he wanted to be a scientist. "What exactly does a scientist do?" I inquired.

"He discovers things, like bones."

"Does that sound like fun to you?" I asked.

"Well, I'm also going to be a psychologist. That's somebody who tells other people what's wrong with them."

"What if I came to you and told you I was always afraid, that I felt as if people were watching me and following me everywhere I went?"

Without hesitation, Willie pointed to his buddy Tarris. "I'd tell you to go see Tarris. He going to be a policeman when he grow up."

❖❖❖ "I want to be a dentist when I grow up," said Ralph.

"Why?"

"I love to pull teeth."

"Do you pull a lot of teeth?" I asked.

Ralph nodded and motioned toward the boy next to him. His friend smiled, revealing a mouth with six or seven teeth missing.

"He did it," was all he said.

❖❖❖ Jonathan told me he was going to be a pilot. "I'll fly an F-16 bomber."

"Won't that mean you'll have to drop bombs? Wouldn't that make you feel bad, dropping bombs on people?"

"I won't drop them on people, just on cities," he explained.

"But what if you bomb people by mistake?" I asked.

"Then I wouldn't look."

❖❖❖ "I'm going to be a paramedic and a writer," said a third-grader.

"What's a paramedic do?" I asked.

"I'll wait until somebody gets sick enough to pass out. Then I go there in an ambulance and write about it."

❖❖❖ Natalie also wanted to be an author, but she had one major reservation. "I'd like to be an author," she said, "but you have to be dead."

❖❖❖ I asked April, another aspiring author, what she felt the hardest part about being a writer would be.

"That's easy," she answered. "Your hands always hurt from writing so much."

❖❖❖ Many wanted to become policemen and policewomen. "What would the hardest part of the job be for a policeman?" I asked.

"Bad people with drugs coming back after you. Two boys killed a policeman in front of my house."

"And you still want to be a policeman?"

"Uh-huh."

❖❖❖ "What do you think would be the hardest part of the job for a policeman?" I asked another second-grader.

"Taking drug dealers to jail."

"What if some bad guy didn't want to go to jail?"

"I'd shoot him."

"What if it was a bad but beautiful woman?"

"I'd take her out."

"Take her out?"

"Yeah, to dinner."

❖❖❖ "What do you think is the hardest part of a policewoman's job, Seneca?"

"Catching robbers if they run. I don't like to run."

❖❖❖ Shamanique said she wanted to be either a cop or a policewoman.

"What's the difference between a cop and a policewoman?" I asked.

"A cop kills people with a gun. A policewoman beats them with a club."

❖❖❖ And there were those who pursued the less sought-after jobs.

"I want to be a farmer," said a first-grade boy who couldn't have lived farther from farmland.

"What do farmers do all day?" I queried.

"They trade animals all day long—chickens for cows, cows for horses, like that."

❖❖❖ "I'm going to be a store cash register. I love the part where they get to help put the stickers on everything. I had stickers once, and I got in trouble because I put them on everything."

❖❖❖ "I'm going to be a teacher," said one first-grader.

"What's the biggest problem a teacher has?"

"Losing her voice. They yell all the time."

❖❖❖ Sharyi knew what she wanted to be when she grew up. "I be a principal."

"How would you run things differently if you ran this school?" I asked.

"I'd let kids talk in the lunchroom. I'd buy jump ropes to play with. And I'd fix the broken things. And no more rats."

Five- and six-year-olds are usually quick to answer the question "What do you want to be when you grow up?" When I quizzed a roomful of kindergartners, they shouted their aspirations:

"Ballerina!"

"Doctor!"

"Fireman!"

"Teacher!"

"President!"

One little five-year-old girl sat quietly at the end of the table. "And what do you want to be when you grow up?" I asked.

She looked around, then leaned over and whispered in my ear. "I want to be four."

"Why do you want to be four?" I asked.

"Because I don't want to grow old." And after a moment's reflection she added, "Four was a very good year for me."

One five-year-old boy had been asked once too often what he wanted to be when he grew up. He set his jaw and answered, "I'm going to be a plain old man."

Applying their own brand of logic, children often imitate the adult world without ever realizing what they're imitating. Natalie's home was filled with modern technology of the information age to which both her parents belonged. In a realm of fax machines and answering machines, Natalie, a second-grader, rarely received a phone call.

Yet one day as she played intently with her brother in the basement, she heard her mother holler, "Natalie, phone for you."

Stunned, unsure how she should respond, she remained silent.

Again came the word: "Natalie, phone call for you."

Finally, after a brief conference, the children yelled up the stairs, "Take a message. Natalie is playing."

Some of Art Linkletter's favorite scenarios posed the child as doctor, with himself as patient. I tried similar tactics with groups of kids ages five to eight across the United States.

Question: What would you do if I came into your office with a broken arm?

❖❖❖ "You'd have to wait your turn, you know."

❖❖❖ "First I'd make you write out a bunch of papers," answered Lisa, tugging one of the brown braids that reached almost to her waist.

"But my arm is broken. I can't write," I protested.

"Well, then, your mother would have to do it."

"I came in all by myself, and I can't write because my arm is broken."

"Well, you shoulda thought of that before you came in."

Thankfully, some of my would-be doctors showed a bit more compassion.

❖❖❖ "I'd put a Band-Aid on it," said five-year-old, blonde, blue-eyed Betsy.

"And if I came in with a broken nose?"

"I'd ask you how you broke your nose. Then I'd put a Band-Aid on it."

"What if I told you my little brother gave me the broken nose?"

"I'd tell you to bring your little brother in, and I'd Band-Aid up his hands."

Question: What would you do if I came in with a broken finger?

❖❖❖ "I'd sew it back on for you," Harold promised.

"And if I came in with a broken arm?"

"I'd sew it back on for you."

"A broken leg?"

"I'd sew it back on for you."

"What if I came in with a broken heart?"

"I'd tell you to cheer up."

Question: What if I came to you with a high fever?

❖❖❖ "I'd give you some medicine," said Joe, who plans to be a doctor.

One of his classmates objected strenuously. "You can't go around giving people medicine. My mom drank too much medicine and had to go to the hospital."

"I'd give her just a little medicine," Joe prescribed.

"You can't do that," accused another classmate. "Medicine is like drugs. And drugs can kill you."

"I'd give you a pill?" Joe suggested softly.

"My sister tried to eat a pill and she almost choked to death until my aunt hit her on the back really hard," still another classmate informed us.

We all looked to poor Joe to get out of that one. After a moment of silence Joe announced, "I'm going to be an animal doctor."

When I complained of a backache, I got immediate sympathy, including one little girl's version of a back rub. I was told to take aspirin, Tylenol, and Advil. After I thanked them all for their help, I asked, "If my back still aches when I get home, what should I do?"

"See if your husband can crack it for you," suggested the girl with the back rub.

"Get your kids to do all your work," offered another.

"Do sit-ups, and then go to the hall closet, under the pillows, and take out the heating pad," said a third.

I needed only three minutes in a northern kindergarten class to pick out the class clown. Jeremy had a variety of comedy monologues and an array of jokes waiting for a straight man.

"Jeremy," I asked, "if you were a doctor, what would you do for me if I came to you with a stomachache?"

"I'd send you home with drugs and tell you to take two and call me in the morning."

"What if I called in the middle of the night and I still had the stomachache?"

"I'd be mad at you for waking me up. And I'd tell you to take more drugs and call me in the morning—but not too early."

"Okay. So in the morning, I call you and say I still have a stomachache."

"I tell you to take lots of drugs. Then don't call us. We'll call you."

Question: Do you have any sound medical advice to give to everybody?

❖❖❖ "Yes," said Chase. "Whenever you have a car accident, you should drive directly to the hospital."

❖❖❖ "Stop smoking and drinking and fighting," said Percy, first grade. "And when you get on a scale, it shouldn't come so far up."

❖❖❖ "Eat strong foods," said Melissa.

❖❖❖ "No bat fights!" Kelly warned. "You'll get hurt and end up in a detention home."

❖❖❖ "Don't eat potato chips!"

"Why not?" I asked.

"Because I knew a guy who ate potato chips and died of salt."

❖❖❖ "Pop's not good for you. So only drink milk or water or Diet Pepsi."

❖❖❖ Christa spoke in a motherly tone. "What's important," she said, "is this. If you are hurt, just calm down. Calm down and try to act normal. Try to be normal. This is very important."

Art Linkletter, in *Kids Say the Darndest Things,* liked to ask children for definitions of professions and vocations. I tried some of the same questions on today's five- and six-year-olds.

Question: What does a nun do?

❖❖❖ "Sells nuts."

❖❖❖ "Nothing."

❖❖❖ "They pray and touch people and work special things."

❖❖❖ "Nuns don't get married," said one kindergarten gal. "And that's why they call them nuns, because they can't have children either."

But Christa disagreed. "They can too get married if they want to. It's a free world, you know."

Question: What does a preacher do?

❖❖❖ "He talks about God, but don't ask me what he says."

❖❖❖ "Crawls around on the ground. They're usually, like, scary, or they sneak into your house."

But his classmates were quick to jump on him and protest that preachers don't do any of those things.

"Oh yeah," he quietly conceded, "I thought you meant *creatures*."

Question: What does a stockbroker do?

❖❖❖ "He takes things up and brings them down again."

❖❖❖ "Breaks houses."

❖❖❖ "It's a robber."

❖❖❖ "Helps people who get shot."

Question: What's insurance?

❖❖❖ "It's when you get paid every day for having people die."

❖❖❖ "People pay it to the bank for workers who build houses."

❖❖❖ "I don't know. But if you don't have it for your car and you get hurt in an accident, you really wish you had some."

Question: What does a lawyer do?

❖❖❖ "A lawyer? He makes strings."

❖❖❖ "He handles cases after the police put them in jail."

❖❖❖ "Works a lot in an office with a briefcase."

❖❖❖ "He sues people for money—like grounding grown-ups."

"And what's an attorney?" I asked the same kids.
"When you turn until you get dizzy."
"It's when you own your own station wagon."

Question: What's an anesthesiologist?

❖❖❖ "Hmmmm. I had it in my mind, and now I forget."

❖❖❖ "It's something slimy and gooey."

❖❖❖ "It has to do with brushing your teeth."

Question: What's the perfect age?

❖❖❖ "Five. Because that's when your brain learns the best. I'm six and I know about these things."

❖❖❖ "Fifteen. My brother is fifteen."

"Why is that such a great age?"

"Because you can do worse things than when you were six, but you never get caught."

❖❖❖ "Twenty is good. You can get married and get a job." She stopped and looked down at her desk. "Maybe six is better."

❖❖❖ "It's good to be one year old," Mary Ellen said in a quiet voice. "When you're one, you get held by your mom and dad and grandma. When you're big, you just get tired legs."

❖❖❖ "I'd like to be fourteen and go to the ninth grade," said an eight-year-old without any hesitation. "Then I could boss my sister around—she's ten. My other age is sixteen, so I can drive. And when I grow up, I'll be a cop, so I can drive really fast without getting arrested."

❖❖❖ "I want to be one year old," said Holly, surprising her classmates. "I just loved drinking from a bottle."

❖❖❖ "One hundred—and get a little respect for a change."

❖❖❖ "I want to be twelve," said a very small eight-year-old boy. "Then I'll have to be bigger than this."

❖❖❖ "I want to be two thousand years old. Then I'd be famous."

❖❖❖ "Sixteen. Then you're sweet and can kiss."

❖❖❖ "A hundred. Then I'll be too old to work or go to school."

❖❖❖ Several children opted for ages under four so they wouldn't have to go to school. One eight-year-old had another motivation. "I want to be four months old. That's the perfect age for spoiling."

When I asked kids, "When do people grow old?", answers ranged from "twelve" to "seventy," but most kids specified the twenties, thirties, and forties.

Question: What happens when people get that old?

❖❖❖ In a third-grade classroom, all hands went up at once and waved furiously.

"Gray hairs! Everywhere!"

"No hairs! Anywhere!"

"Their skin wrinkles up."

"They get smaller."

"They get crippled."

"You get fat."

"They stop shaving."

"Your chin sags way down into your neck. And it sags into your collar."

"You get more pains than any other people."

❖❖❖ One group of second-graders began talking about old people.

"They lose their hearing," Alan told us.

"Why do you think they lose their hearing?" I asked.

"They're not used to kids yelling all day anymore," he said.

"Huh-uh," said Maggie. "Wax buildup. Or their ears are just worn out from listening to so many things all those years."

"Noise pollution," came yet another explanation. This one seemed to satisfy everyone and ended the discussion.

Grandma told Michael, four years old, that she was going to drive Great-grandma to the store to do some shopping.

"She doesn't drive because she's old," he commented.

"That's right," Grandma said.

"Did she drive when she was new?" came the logical follow-up.

Lee tried to fill in his grandmother after his first day at kindergarten. "I think the teacher's old, Grandma, 'cause she has wrinkled elbows like you."

Question: Why do older people lose their hair?

❖❖❖ "When they were young," said Brandon, "they were hippies and they shaved their heads once too much."

❖❖❖ Charlotte had a different idea, which had to be coaxed out of her by her classmates after she started and then stopped. "Okay," she said. "They lose their hair because they made out too much when they were our age."

Question: Why do old people have wrinkled skin?

❖❖❖ A brown-eyed first-grader with long, blonde hair answered with a question in her voice: "Because they stayed in the bathtub too long?"

"No," John said, laughing at his classmate's answer. "Their skin wrinkles when they shrink. It doesn't fit them anymore, and the wrinkles are left-over skin."

When three-year-old Maggie got mad at her grandmother, she shouted, "I'm really mad at you. And anyway, you have cracks from the top of your head to the tip of your toes!"

In his journal for his 4-H creative arts project, Tom wrote: "I helped my mom for a week. She's not old or disabled. She just has a lot to do."

Question: How can you tell when someone is really old?

❖❖❖ "They start to get uglier about thirty-five or forty years old," Jeremiah said. "And then they smell."

❖❖❖ "They become old geezers," Tim said.

"What exactly is a geezer?" I asked.

"You know," he continued, "scrunched back; can't get around like he used to do; hair falls out. And that makes them mean."

❖❖❖ "They play bingo all day."

❖❖❖ "They lie on the couch all day long and eat Doritos."

❖❖❖ "Old people begin dressing weird, and they can't swing high on swings," said Alicia.

❖❖❖ "They whistle while they talk."

❖❖❖ "When they get really old, they act like they're going to talk before they really talk, like the mouth moves first, before the words come out."

❖❖❖ "Getting old isn't so bad," said Dan, a fourth-grader. "It's later. After you get old, you get rotten and die."

After such dismal descriptions of old age, I felt I needed to follow up on the subject.

Question: Why do you think people get old?

❖❖❖ "Glands," said a fourth-grader.

❖❖❖ "If you never grow old," said a fresh-faced boy, "you'll *never* be able to grow a beard."

❖❖❖ Trynia made a good point: "If nobody got old, we'd all be kids, and we'd all look just alike."

One of her classmates took it a bit further: "If our parents had stayed kids, none of us would be here!"

❖❖❖ "Who would go see the movies that you have to be over eighteen to see?" asked one practical third-grade girl.

❖❖❖ "We have to make room for new people," explained another third-grader. "So we gotta get old and die. Besides, God would get awful lonely if nobody went up to heaven to live with him."

❖❖❖ But the last word came from a third-grade class philosopher: "People get older because they live longer. As time grows old, we grow old. And that's it."

Seven-year-old Justin's great-grandparents came to visit. Justin was happy to see them, but his dog Molly was not. She barked at them the whole time. Finally Great-grandma said, "Gee, Molly must not like us, Justin."

Justin tried to reassure her: "Don't worry, Grammy. She just doesn't like old people."

In one second-grade discussion about old age, Amanda said she knew a secret. "Sometimes old people try to look like young people," she whispered.

"Yeah," Tony agreed. "They put on all this makeup and hairspray, and color their hair, and wear stylish clothes, and listen to rap music."

"What else do they do to look young?" I probed.

"Some old people drink ten glasses of water a day, move their skin around, go to tanning beds, drive better cars, and use skin bracer. If that doesn't work, they go to the beach and to the circus and talk about popping zits."

"They get their faces lifted by plastic surgery, buy false teeth, and move to a warm place," Amanda concluded.

"What does the saying 'Life begins at forty' mean?"

One disgruntled second-grader was quick to tell me: "Forty o'clock. Life begins after they send us to bed."

✹ *CHAPTER 9* ✹

Men and Women/ Love and Marriage

Go see a girl? I'd rather smell a skunk!
—Beaver Cleaver, on "Leave it to Beaver"

From the time they are very young, little girls seem on the verge of becoming women. Sitting in a bathtub full of warm water and bubbles, four-year-old Angie declared, "It feels so good to be a woman."

One evening as little Valerie was bathing, she asked her mother, "Can I shave my legs?"

"You're much too young to shave your legs," Mother told her.

"Well then, will you do it for me?" came the reply.

Four-year-old Gretchen watched as Mother tried to put on false eyelashes. After several attempts, much muttering, and successive squirts of adhesive, Mother stopped, then started again. Gretchen stared in awe at this bizarre ritual of her gender, and commented, "God must sure have a lot of glue."

Question: What makes a real woman?

❖❖❖ "Lipstick and earrings." (Katy, third grade)

❖❖❖ "A job, makeup, and responsibility." (Amy, eleven)

❖❖❖ "When you can have a baby." (Elizabeth, eight)

❖❖❖ "When you know the answer to this question." (Jenny, twelve)

❖❖❖ A fourth-grade boy considered this question seriously, then answered: "It's the shape of her hair."

"What shape is the hair of a real woman?" I queried.

"It's something that happens to the hair when they get about eighteen."

Intrigued, I continued. "Well, what happens?"

"I don't know yet," he said. "I'm only nine."

❖❖❖ "You're a real woman," said one third-grade boy, "when you can make promises, give allowances, and marry the boss."

❖❖❖ "You have to be able to pay bills and be marriable."

❖❖❖ "When they're sexy for guys," said Daisy, second grade.

Question: What's "sexy?"

❖❖❖ "I don't know. Something to do with the body. But you have to be careful because you can get AIDS."

❖❖❖ "It's when you roll on somebody."

❖❖❖ "I know how to be sexy. Be on a diet."

❖❖❖ "It happens when it gets dark. I hate sexy."

❖❖❖ "If they give me sex at school," said a second-grade boy, "I'll stay home."

❖❖❖ "It's when the man goes out and hunts a wild animal and kills it and brings it home to the woman and she cooks it. That's sexy."

Jason, who loved to color and resented the small, eight-crayon box his mother sent him off to school with, tried to make his mother understand which of his first-grade classmates he was talking about. "Cindy!" he repeated, frustrated.

"Well," Mother suggested, "describe her for me."

Jason thought about it, then complied: "Blonde and sixty-four Crayolas."

Question: What makes a real man?

❖❖❖ "It takes forever," said Jennifer. "My dad still isn't there."

"What do you mean?"

"Sometimes he pours whole, huge glassfuls of water over his head just to make us laugh."

❖❖❖ "No man ever grows up," Amy commented, shaking her head.

❖❖❖ "Size and muscles."

❖❖❖ "When he can protect a woman, he's a man—about twenty-five years old."

❖❖❖ But two fourth-grade boys had the most thoughtful answers: "If he has him an education, a job, and he's smart" and "If he helps raise his kids, that makes him a real man."

Alison, age four, always slept with one leg under the covers and one leg out. Finally, her parents asked her why she slept this way. "Because Mom is cold-blooded and Dad is hot-blooded," came the logical answer.

When I asked third-graders if boys or girls matured faster, I created quite a stir. And although the answers usually aligned by gender, there were exceptions.

"Women mature faster," said Erica, "because they can have babies."

"Men mature faster," said a male classmate. "My dad knows more than my mom. Every time you ask her something, she says, 'Go ask your dad.' "

"If it weren't for us," said a female, "you boys wouldn't even be here."

"No," objected a male classmate, "men do because they're smarter."

"How do you know they're smarter?" I asked.

"No girl has ever become a president, has she?"

William braved a comment on the other side. "Women mature faster, because men don't really care."

Nine-year-old Joey hovered over his little sister Lisa and threatened, "I'm gonna give you a knuckle sandwich!"

Lisa, hands on hips in the little-woman fashion that only a six-year-old can affect, yelled back at him: "You probably don't even know how to make one!"

"Ever go on a date?" I asked two kindergarten students.

"Not me," said the first. "I'm not even married."

"Me neither," answered the second, "but I know what they are. You go camping and go to bed."

Question: How can you tell if a boy/girl likes you?

❖❖❖ "That's easy," Erica told me. "If he sits down with you on the bus, then he stays there a long time, when he could have moved to a different seat. And if one of his friends yells for him to sit with them, and he still doesn't move, then he loves you."

❖❖❖ "I can always tell when a girl likes me," said Dominic. "She gets this look like she's sick, but sick and happy. That's how you know. That look."

❖❖❖ "When a boy likes you," said Tina, second grade, "he messes with you. He pulls your hair or steals your pencil or hits you on top of the head—something like that."

❖❖❖ "Girls stare at you when they like you. And some girls, they scoot their chairs closer to you. Those are the ones you have to watch out for."

❖❖❖ "First they talk to you. Then you act like you don't like each other. Then one thing leads to another, and you're going together."

Question: How would you know you were in love?

❖❖❖ "Someone kisses you. They don't just do that unless they're in love," Dean told me.

"That's not true," objected Alicia.

"Well, how do you know you're in love?" I asked Alicia.

"They have to kiss and hug you. Then you know."

❖❖❖ "If they flirt with you, they love you," said Melody.

"How do boys flirt?" I asked.

"They stay real shy and stop talking whenever you walk by them. And when you're not looking, they stare at you."

"How do you know they're staring at you if you're not looking?"

"Your friends tell you."

❖❖❖ "You know if they ask you to marry them."

❖❖❖ "If he gives you flowers, a hundred rings, Valentine Day hearts when it isn't even Valentine's and he doesn't have to, and then a wedding dress. Then he loves you."

❖❖❖ "It goes like this," five-year-old Todd explained. "First, I'm just curious. Then I'm a friend. Then I'm a boyfriend. Then I'm married. Then . . . No, that's all."

❖❖❖ "It's when your eyes lock together," Erin said.

❖❖❖ "Boys don't talk to you unless they're really cracking on you," another informed me.

❖❖❖ "They buy you something, or it's like *Beauty and the Beast* with music."

❖❖❖ "I'm not sure when I like them," said Erica. "But I'm sure when they like me."

"How are you sure?" I asked.

"Two disgusting kisses."

❖❖❖ "I have to tell you," one first-grade lad admitted. "Nobody knows much about love really."

I'm not sure I was quite ready for some of the contemporary answers I received when I posed the following question.

Question: Do you want to get married?

❖❖❖ "I never want to get married," Lea said.

"Why not?"

"Because the man might drink drugs. And then he would get AIDS. And then I would get it too and die. You never know."

❖❖❖ "I want to get married," Charlotte announced. "Then I can go on a honeymoon."

"What would you do on a honeymoon?"

She lowered her voice so only I could hear: "Go to a restaurant and drink wine."

❖❖❖ "I don't want to get married because sooner or later you end up with a baby in your stomach. Then you have to go to the doctor and get it out. And I hate to go to the doctor."

❖❖❖ "Yes," Robert answered softly and dreamily.

"Why"

" 'Cause then you got you one person who love you for sure."

❖❖❖ "Sure," said Stanley. "I want to get married. Then I get my wife to get her a good job. And I can lay on the couch and watch TV all day while she work."

❖❖❖ "Yes, I guess," Michelle said reluctantly. "If he stays quiet and won't say anything and gives me twins when I want them and fixes my food."

❖❖❖ "No sir!" said Jolita. "I'm not getting married!"

"Why not?"

"Because there's sex and AIDS."

❖❖❖ "I'm not getting married because I'm going to live with my parents forever," said Roslyn.

I'd been talking with students in inner-city Los Angeles, and many of the stories I'd heard had been sad. So I was thrilled with what seemed to be a positive response to my question.

"You must really like it at home," I encouraged.

"Well," Roslyn explained, "if you be the wife, then you can get yourself beat on. But the man don't usually beat on the kids, 'specially the girls. So I plan on staying the girl, and not the wife."

❖❖❖ "The only reason I might get married is 'cause I'm going to have me some kids. And I think you need a husband. I keep asking my mama where babies come from, but she says that's none of my business. So far, I know they come from a seed in your tummy. But I can't figure how they get it out."

❖❖❖ "I'll never get married," said a cute second-grade girl.

"Why not?"

"Men!" she said. "They think they're kings."

❖❖❖ Many of the boys wanted to get married.

"I'll be a scientist and have ten kids and come home every day at eleven in the morning to play with them."

"Yep," said another boy. "Wives have to cook and clean and take care of the kids. I'm going to get me a wife."

Alfred was a bit more cautious. "I'll get married," he said, "but first she'll have to sign a paper that says if I divorce her, she won't get anything."

❖❖❖ "Nobody's going to get me to marry them," said Ryan. "I hate girls. They scream all the time. They pick on you. Babies make me sick. And I don't have room for anybody else in my house."

❖❖❖ "Marriage," asserted Leo, "is stress."

❖❖❖ "I'm getting married," Joseph said, ignoring peer pressure from his two male companions. "Girls are very pretty. I'll take my wife to St. Louis in a truck for our honeymoon and I'll buy her three CDs."

❖❖❖ "I'll never get married."

"Why not?"

"Just one more pesky boy around the house."

Question: What should you know about a person before you agree to marry him or her?

❖❖❖ "Does he have his own bankbook and one for you?"

❖❖❖ "If he has HIV."

❖❖❖ "Yeah, if he has that disease thing." And everyone helped out: "AIDS!"

❖❖❖ "Does he smoke cigarettes?"

"And what if he does smoke cigarettes?" I asked.

"Then you have to tell him to stop it."

"But what if he won't stop smoking?"

"Then you dump him," she said simply.

❖❖❖ "You need to ask him how many kids he has."

❖❖❖ "You gotta ask her if she's already married 'cause they can put you in jail for that."

❖❖❖ "Before you marry somebody," Lisa told us, "you have to know each other well."

"That's very wise," I said. "How can you know when you know each other well enough?"

"You buy a magazine and pass a quiz on each other. That's what my mama did."

❖❖❖ "If you want to be safe and marry somebody," said one third-grade girl, "you should watch him play with your kids. Watch him real close. Then you'll know if he's good for marrying."

"Or," said a friend, "if he has kids already and treats them bad."

❖❖❖ "You have to know about his whole life," one first-grade girl said seriously.

"For example . . ." I prompted.

"For example," she continued, "his attitude, his background, his parents, police record."

Her girlfriend then joined in: "You need to know his health care and his life insurance policy."

"What does health care mean?" I probed.

The first girl responded: "Does baldness run in his family and like that."

❖❖❖ Another group of second-graders decided that the most important thing you had to be sure of before you married somebody was that the person loved you. "How can you be sure he or she loves you?" I asked.

"If he goes away, and you miss him, that's a good love test."

"And," added another girl, "if he writes you letters. Because if he goes away and says he's missing you, but he doesn't write you any letters, he might not still love you."

Question: What does a guy have to do or have before you'll marry him?

❖❖❖ "A good last name."

❖❖❖ "Proof that he's not just using me to get even with some old girlfriend."

❖❖❖ "He has to prove that he's divorced and not still secretly married."

❖❖❖ "He has to promise not to date anyone else."

❖❖❖ "He has to have a swimming pool in his backyard."

A four-year-old girl ran into the house one day. "Mom! Mom! Ryan asked me to marry him!"

"Well, what did you say?" Mom asked.

"I told him I'd have to ask my mother first."

✸ *CHAPTER 10* ✸

Geographically Speaking

All the world's a stage.
—William Shakespeare, *As You Like It*

Geography questions revealed more than a few misconceptions.

Question: *What's geography?*

When I asked five-year-olds, the question was usually greeted with silence, but a few brave souls dared definitions.

❖❖❖ "It's like jogging? Yes, something to do with jogging."

❖❖❖ "The same thing as lethargy."

❖❖❖ "It has to do with jobs."

Question: How big is America?

❖❖❖ Three kindergarten buddies tackled this one.

"This big!" answered Janine, extending her arms as wide as she could.

"This big!" said Adam, stretching his arms further apart than Janine's.

Only Dennis remained, and he was the smallest of the three. I watched as he studied Janine's measurement, then Adam's. Finally he grinned up at me, hands firmly in his lap. "Bigger than both their arms put together."

Question: Which is the biggest state in the United States?

❖❖❖ "Europe," said five-year-old Anita. Then she looked to her friends to back her up.

"Yeah, Europe," they all chimed in.

"Who told you Europe was the biggest state in the United States?" I asked them.

In unison came the telling answer: "Our teacher!"

❖❖❖ One Ohio first-grader had a different idea about the largest state.

"Ohio is the biggest state," she declared. "In fact, it's almost as big as America and the oceans put together."

"How do you know this?" I asked.

"In our book, the United States takes up one page, and on the other page is Ohio. And they both take up about a page."

❖❖❖ "The biggest state," Leroy said confidently, "is Chicago."

"No sir!" said Waltia. "It's . . . Africa."

"Florida!" "Washington, D.C.!" "New York!" "America!" came the responses from Leroy's classmates.

Leroy wasn't shaken, though. "The biggest state is still Chicago," he repeated. "My daddy told me so, and he's bigger than your daddy."

And that was the end of that discussion.

The Sunday-school teacher asked four-year-old Scott if he had ever been to Kentucky. Quickly he replied, "Yes, 'Tucky Fried Chicken, Wendy's, and McDonald's!"

Question: What's the smallest state in the United States?

❖❖❖ "Texas."

"China."

"Hawaii."

"America."

"Jamaica."

"Puerto Rico, my country!" shouted Juan.

I studied the seven- and eight-year-olds before me. "Now, you can't all be right. Who really knows?"

Juan was the first to stake his claim. "It's Puerto Rico," he promised me. "I know it is the smallest state."

"How do you know that, Juan?"

"Because I have never been there. And everywhere I have been, has been very big."

One kindergartner was tired of seeing his mom spend so much time with his big brother as they studied each night, memorizing the state capitals. Finally he decided he could play this game too. "Mommy! Mommy!" he cried, running in from the backyard and interrupting his brother's recitation. "What's the capital of Tree?"

"I don't know, honey," his mom admitted. "What is the capital of Tree?"

"T!"

I asked one group of second-graders to tell me everything they'd learned about other countries.

"In French, they speak Chinese," asserted the first young man at the table. "And that means they call their teacher 'saint.' "

"I know how to speak a . . . what-do-you-call-it? . . . another language," Caleb said. "I forget which language it is. But I know a song about it. I think it's Hawaii."

"I went to China!" shouted a classmate. But when we all turned to focus on him, he added, "I don't think I really did."

In another second-grade class, Ryan wanted to tell us his discovery about other lands. "You won't believe this," he began, "but in California they speak American just like us."

One little kindergartner, proud of her Italian heritage, missed her mom and wasn't faring too well the first week of school. Other, more streetwise kids saw her as an easy target. "Hey! I saw your mommy out in the hall," one would say. But when she ran to the hall, the hall was empty and the room filled with chuckles.

One particular classmate was relentless in his harassment. "Your mother left and she's never coming back," he taunted.

"Yes she is."

"No she's not," he insisted. He kept it up throughout the day until he grew tired of the game. "Okay," he admitted. "She's coming back. I was only teasing."

But she was not going to let him get away that easily. "In Italian," she told him, "we call that lying."

During a drive to view the Christmas lights, it was necessary to travel a dark, winding road. Five-year-old Scott broke the silence: "Well, that's what I call a crooked mile."

Question: Where would you go if you could go anywhere in the world?

❖❖❖ "Home," said a sad-looking kindergarten boy. It was the only word I was to get from him all day.

❖❖❖ "I'd go out to dinner," said Waltia, a second-grader in a city school.

"Out to dinner where?" I asked.

"To Ponderosa for Chinese food."

❖❖❖ "I'd go to New Jersey," Jared said with a trace of an East Coast accent.

"Why New Jersey?"

"Because they have the whole entire ocean, and other places just have some of it."

❖❖❖ "To the Bahamas," said a tanned six-year-old. "Mommy and I went there and we left Daddy at home so we could have more fun."

❖❖❖ "I would go to Hawaii," Ralph answered, "where the volcanoes grow and the lava flows."

❖❖❖ "Californ-i-a." Omar appeared worried when the other three first-graders at our table didn't immediately agree with him. "You can surf there all day and night." And since he was still met with unimpressed stares, he added, "Even Santa Claus goes there in the summer."

❖❖❖ "I'd go to India," said five-year-old Kimberly.

"Where is India?" I asked, surprised that she was familiar with the country.

"India is on the other side of the clouds, where the moon and sun go when they go down behind the clouds every day."

"I see. What would you see there?"

"Indians, of course."

❖❖❖ Martin didn't really want to go anywhere special . . . again. "I've already been to the place I wanted to go most in the world," he told me.

"Tell me about it."

"Well," and he sighed, as if recalling every detail. "I went there with Bambi." Another pause as he stared far away. "We sat under palm trees and drank cold drinks with straws that had lots of bends in them. And we sat in our swimsuits by a big swimming pool."

"You and Bambi?" I asked.

"That's what I said, me and Bambi."

"Can you describe Bambi for me?" I ventured.

"Big, brown eyes, kinda short, brownish hair. You know—Bambi. Her mother got killed by a hunter."

❖❖❖ "I know where I want to go," said a serious Katie. "I want to go to heaven!"

"Why do you want to go to heaven?" I asked.

"Because I sure don't want to go to . . ." and here she whispered, ". . . *that other place*!"

Question: What would I see if I went to Washington, D.C.?

Midwestern first-graders had definite ideas about their nation's capital.

❖❖❖ "Lots of money," Ryan answered. "And great big rocks."

"Big rocks? Like monuments?" I asked.

"No, not that. Big rocks with faces on them. Faces of presidents."

❖❖❖ "In Washington, D.C.," Adam told me, "you'd see a blue house."

"He means the White House," Ryan corrected.

"Oops," Adam muttered. "Well, it should be blue. White is boring."

❖❖❖ "All the president's men!" Evan answered.

One little guy couldn't wait to tell his teacher that he had taken an exciting vacation over spring break.

"Where did you go?" the teacher asked him.

"I went to Florida!" he said proudly.

"That's nice. And where did you stay?"

"I stayed with my grandmother in a condom."

Question: ***Would you like to go to the moon someday?***

Preschoolers weren't so sure about moon travel.

❖❖❖ "Only if I went with an adult," Nathan said. "It would be too easy to get lost."

❖❖❖ "I don't want to go to the moon," Adam told me. "It would be too easy to fall off and bang up your knee."

❖❖❖ "Well, I'll go," Michelle said.

"Good for you, Michelle. Why do you want to go to the moon?"

"Because it's better than the sun. If I went to the sun, I might burn my feet."

Question: ***Where do tornadoes come from?***

❖❖❖ "The basement," came the answer from a first-grade boy.

"From the basement?" I repeated.

"Yeah. Like worms, from lettuce."

❖❖❖ "Tornado drills cause them; they shake up the earth."

Question: ***Where do earthquakes come from?***

❖❖❖ "Straight from the world," Manny said.

❖❖❖ Sierra let me in on a secret: "They come from the devil. He real mad at God and us and makes earth swallow us."

❖❖❖ "Earthquakes are when God gets mad and jumps around."

Question: Where do mountains come from?

❖❖❖ "Seeds."

❖❖❖ "Big ice cream cones dropped upside down by giants."

Question: Why is the sea salty?

❖❖❖ "Salt ships spilled."

❖❖❖ "Leeches."

❖❖❖ "A pipeline broke in Alaska."

❖❖❖ "Salt rains."

❖❖❖ "When God made a flood a long time ago, he flavored it."

Question: Where does the sun go when the sun goes down?

❖❖❖ "It goes from our house, to America, to Africa, and back to our house again."

❖❖❖ "It doesn't really go anywhere," confided Jamie. "It's just that you can't see it anymore when it gets too dark outside."

❖❖❖ "First it goes behind the clouds," Marinda explained, using her hands and arms and whole body to illustrate. "Then it goes down into the ground and waits until morning. Then, when it's really early in the morning, it pops back up into space."

❖❖❖ "I'll tell you a secret if you want to know," Sharita said quietly.

I assured her I did.

"Okay. The sun doesn't really go down. We go up."

Since young children live in a world of their own, they are often not fully aware of the larger world adults live in. I tried to get a handle on how children perceive current global struggles by asking them to name three countries the United States considers friends and three we consider enemies. Here's a compilation of what they came up with.

Friends	*Enemies*
England	Baghdad
Somalia	Cuba
Russia	Iraq
France	Japan

America
China
Canada
Japan
Germany
Mexico
Turkey
North Pole
Puerto Rico
Cuba
Detroit
Texas
North America
Kansas

Brazil
Hussein
Ethiopia
California
Germany
Vietnam
South Korea
Yugoslavia
Malaysia
Mexico
South America
The U.P.
East America

You may have noticed that some names appear on both sides. Perhaps the kids are more in tune than I imagined.

Question: What's the meanest country?

Here are some typical second-grade responses.

❖❖❖ "Iraq is the meanest."
"Huh-uh! Iran is meaner."

❖❖❖ "I think . . . Baghdad? Yeah, Baghdad."

❖❖❖ "Soviet Union."

❖❖❖ "Ireland. They've been fighting for fifty-six years—each other!"

❖❖❖ "We are the meanest."

"What do you mean?" I asked him.

"We're the biggest and the baddest!" he declared proudly.

Question: What do you know about Russia?

❖❖❖ "Well," began five-year-old Cary, "it's when everybody else is ready and they yell at you to hurry up because you're always the last one."

❖❖❖ Meagan, also age five, had a different idea. "It's like when you're around water and you feel like you're going to fall in, but then you don't. That's it."

Times have changed. Children no longer quake under the fear of impending communism; in fact, most of them didn't know what it was.

Question: What's communism?

❖❖❖ "It's when your head is really dirty and they send you home from school," offered one six-year-old.

"No," said her classmate, "it's when you have really dirty hands."

Those answers came from first-graders. Here's what I got when I asked fourth-graders the same question.

❖❖❖ "It's where one country helps another country."

❖❖❖ "I think it's when people try to run other people's lives and they don't want them to."

❖❖❖ "It's something between Russia and us."

❖❖❖ "It's in a comic strip—something real funny, maybe the name of the comic strip."

Now, after the break-up of the Soviet Union and the fall of the Berlin Wall, how much do children know about the way things were?

Question: What's the Iron Curtain?

❖❖❖ "The Pittsburgh Steelers' front line!"

❖❖❖ "Two countries fighting head-to-head and neither one wants to give up to the other one."

❖❖❖ "A curtain with an iron stuck to it?"

❖❖❖ "It's a house made entirely of iron . . . in Hawaii, I think."

Question: What's the biggest problem facing our world today?

❖❖❖ "Littering."

❖❖❖ "Desert Storm people getting killed in Somalia."

❖❖❖ "Endangered species, like bulls and leopards."

❖❖❖ "Pollution. We need electric cars."

❖❖❖ "People throwing cans and trash in the sea, killing whales, and fish dying."

❖❖❖ "Smoking."

❖❖❖ "Killing people."

The postcard passed along to me by one mom makes me want to compile a book of greetings from camp. Here's what eight-year-old Dan wrote home to his cousin Jim:

Dear Jim

We got raided Monday. One day a kid threw up and some dogs ate it.

Dan

✹ CHAPTER 11 ✹

Hysterical History

Blessed are the young,
For they shall inherit the national debt.
—Herbert Hoover

Kids create their own versions of history; what they don't know for sure, they'll readily make up.

Question: What happened to the dinosaurs?

❖❖❖ "Meteors got 'em."

❖❖❖ "No, they blew up."

❖❖❖ "They were chasing leaves and fell over into a valley and died."

❖❖❖ "It got real hot with no water because all the water fell in the cracks of the earth. And dinosaurs can't live without water."

❖❖❖ "They got too big to be seen in public."

❖❖❖ "They died when people came. It was either them or us."

❖❖❖ "Dinosaur traps," six-year-old Steve asserted in a tone intended to end the discussion.

"Dinosaur traps?" I questioned.

"Yep. They were pretty good, weren't they?"

Question: What was the best thing anyone ever invented?

Some of the kids immediately thought of their favorite places: Disneyland, Hawaii, Pizza Hut. Others had other ideas.

❖❖❖ "Bowling."

❖❖❖ "Roller skates."

❖❖❖ "Candy bars."

❖❖❖ "Other planets."

❖❖❖ "Ponies."

❖❖❖ "Monkey bars."

❖❖❖ "Masterpieces, like statues."

Surprised by such a refined answer from a five-year-old boy in blue jeans and tennis shoes, I queried, "What's your favorite statue?"

"I like all of them," he assured me, "especially the ones with no clothes on."

❖❖❖ Six-year-old Jenna looked dreamily at the handsome boy seated beside her. "The best invention is love, isn't it, Bradley?"

❖❖❖ One little boy surprised me. "The best invention isn't quite finished yet," he answered.

"It isn't?" I asked.

"No. Because I'm building it."

And try as I might, I couldn't get him to reveal what he had in store for the world. My only clue was his answer when I asked what was holding him up, what he needed to finish his invention: "I just need more wheels, more wires, and more space."

Although many kids still think of war as a game, something glorious and exciting, I ran across several children who didn't think war was such a good idea.

"What are wars?" I asked.

Caleb was the first to answer in a room of kindergartners: "It's them . . . them . . . them fighting things."

"War," said an eleven-year-old, "is a waste of ammunition."

Question: Why do grown-ups have wars?

❖❖❖ "Everybody wants everybody's land!" Ryan said. "The cowboys started it when they stole land from the Indians. And everybody's been fighting ever since."

❖❖❖ "Grown-ups argue too much," said one little girl. "And then they start to make fun of each other. And then they fight. And that's war."

❖❖❖ "People from one country always want to destroy people from a different country."

"Why is that?" I asked.

"So that your country can be the only one."

❖❖❖ "You can't have heroes if you don't have wars . . . except I guess you could have heroes if you had fires that guys could run into and save people. . . . But you never know if you're going to be where the fire is."

❖❖❖ "If somebody takes something of yours, like water, you can have a war with them. But if you're a kid and somebody takes your water, that's just sharing."

❖❖❖ Casper had the simplest answer: "Everybody wants to win."

Question: Has America ever lost a war?

❖❖❖ "Probably," Julie answered, disappointment tingeing her voice. "Everybody has to lose sometimes."

❖❖❖ Aaron was certain of his answer: "Yes! We lost."

"Who did America lose a war to?" I pressed.

"China . . . and French."

"No sir!" "We did not, Aaron!" said his buddies.

"Did too!" he responded, unruffled. "It was a tug of war!"

Question: How would you end war?

❖❖❖ "You have to say you're sorry and shake hands and be friends," Heather said.

❖❖❖ "You just stop fighting. Then they'll stop fighting too."

❖❖❖ "You tell Jesus, 'cause if he sees it, he'll stop it with rain and thunder, lightning," Sierra said.

❖❖❖ "You blow the whistle, or tell the police."

❖❖❖ "I think you end it with a flag."

Question: How did our country get started?

❖❖❖ Six-year-old Tina responded immediately: "The Indians started it."

"And then what?" I asked.

"And then the rest of us finished it."

❖❖❖ "Christopher Columbus sailed the ocean blue in 1492 and started America," chanted Erin.

"Why did he do that?" I asked.

"I think he fell in love with some queen and he had to do it to win her over."

Question: How did school start?

❖❖❖ Lester looked at me as if I needed to go back to school.

"With the teacher yelling at us," he said.

"No," I said, trying to clarify. "I mean, how did school begin in the first place, like a really long time ago?"

"Oh," he said, nodding. "With the Letter People."

Question: Tell me some of the most important things that have happened in history.

❖❖❖ "They're all real bad things," Jason said.

"Like what?"

"I don't want to talk about it."

❖❖❖ "Jesus was born," Haley offered.

❖❖❖ "World War I—America versus England. World War II—Asia versus China and the United States."

❖❖❖ "My grandfather fought in World War II. My whole family almost fought in the war—my family against the whole world."

❖❖❖ "Vietnam. We won peace against South America and set it free."

❖❖❖ "Ninja turtles went from cartoons to real people."

❖❖❖ "Martin Luther King got himself shot."

Question: How has life changed from when your parents were kids?

❖❖❖ "All the houses and cars were old then."

❖❖❖ "They hadn't invented games or television yet, so they had to work all the time."

❖❖❖ "It was very dangerous then," said a five-year-old.

"What was so dangerous about life then?"

"Dinosaurs fought night and day," she answered.

Kindergartners had the toughest time picturing what life must have been like when their parents were kids. In fact, many kindergartners couldn't imagine such a thing.

❖❖❖ "*My* mom and dad?" Belinda asked. Then all she and her friend could do was giggle.

❖❖❖ "There were only a couple of toys, no color TV, and no remote cars."

❖❖❖ "Everybody wore bloomers under everything."

❖❖❖ "The whole world listened to Elvis."

❖❖❖ "They could date when they were nine and get married. We can't even kiss on the lips."

❖❖❖ "People were born on kitchen tables."

❖❖❖ "They had sparkly eyeglasses with points on the end."

❖❖❖ "When they got in trouble in school, they got spankings. We just get chairs in the hall."

❖❖❖ "They had to eat macaroni and cheese every day—for every single meal!"

❖❖❖ "They wore ugly clothes, listened to terrible music, and wanted to change everything."

❖❖❖ "They used different years then. They used to keep time different and have different calendars."

CHAPTER 12

Pint-Sized Politics

In America, anyone can become president. That's one of the risks you take.—Adlai Stevenson

One month before the presidential election, I sat with five kindergartners in the back of their classroom.

Question: Does anybody know what politics means?

❖❖❖ Silence.

"Any ideas?"

Finally a little girl with a brown ponytail said, "I think they're little bugs that stick to your hair when you go camping."

Most of the kids I talked with during election year were really into the struggle and drama of politics, having definite ideas about how they'd cast their votes and which party they'd support.

Question: What's the difference between Republicans and Democrats?

❖❖❖ "They have two different animals representing them," said a third-grader. "Donkeys and elephants."

"My mother calls one by the real name," said a classmate, "and the other one by a name she shouldn't call it and I can't even say."

"Republicans call everybody else names," said another.

❖❖❖ "Democrats won, and Republicans didn't."

❖❖❖ "Republicans usually win."

❖❖❖ "One's been in before; one's in now."

❖❖❖ "Democrats like abortions."

❖❖❖ "Republicans have more money."

❖❖❖ "Democrats spend more money."

❖❖❖ "Democrats have to be younger."

❖❖❖ "There's no difference at all."

"Then why do we have two political parties?" I asked.

"So people will have more than one person to vote for when it's election time."

Question: How do you get to be president of the United States?

❖❖❖ Jeb, a little guy with sharp, blue eyes and blond hair cut Dutch-style, claimed to know all about presidents because his dad knew all there was to know about presidents: "If you want to be a president, you have to get on TV a lot and say stuff about the other guys who want to be president."

"What kind of stuff do you have to say about the other guys?" I asked.

"Mostly the kind of stuff they don't let you say on television."

"How old do you need to be to vote for president?"

"At least fifteen," Jeb assured me, "so you can read the stuff they won't let you put on TV."

"Who would make the best president?" I asked my knowledgeable new friend.

He thought about it. "Well, Bush would make the best president, but he's dead."

My surprise must have been obvious. Jeb looked confused, but only for a second. Then he recovered and repeated his claim. "Yes, he's dead."

"No he's not!" said one of the girls who had been listening to our conversation.

"Yes, he is," countered Jeb.

"No he's not, because I saw him on TV last night!"

Jeb smiled knowingly, patiently. "You can't believe everything you see on TV."

Question: Who would make the best president?

❖❖❖ "President Tubbs, because he was really funny."

"I'm not sure I remember President Tubbs," I admitted.

"He's the one that was so fat he got stuck in a bathtub."

❖❖❖ "President Kennedy. He freed the black slaves."

❖❖❖ "Santa Claus, because he would give us stuff instead of taking everything away."

❖❖❖ "My sister. She's really good at bossing people around."

❖❖❖ "Jesus. He'd love everybody."

❖❖❖ A second-grade boy in an inner-city school said he believed his grandfather would make the best president of the United States. "Why would he make a good president?" I asked.

"Because he don't do drugs and he real old."

❖❖❖ Another second-grader, George, said his grandmother would make the best president "because she don't do nothing except sit and crochet all day. We wouldn't ever have no wars if she was in the White House."

❖❖❖❖❖❖

I visited Sarah's first-grade class on Inauguration Day. "Sarah, what's the inauguration?" I asked her.

"That's easy," she answered. "That's when everybody swears at the new president."

Question: What does the president do all day?

I asked a small group of kindergartners this question when I visited a suburban elementary school.

❖❖❖ "That's a good question," said one boy.

I thanked him.

"I know," said Alice, his classmate. "He sits around with papers in his office."

Her girlfriend nodded agreement. "Lots of papers. He looks through them and writes on them and puts them in different order."

❖❖❖ "Works for money."

❖❖❖ "He makes laws every night when everyone else is asleep."

❖❖❖ "I think he works for a year and then tries to make people like him for three years so that he can do it again."

❖❖❖ "He bosses the vice president around all day."

❖❖❖ "He shakes hands with everybody who comes to Washington on a plane."

Answers to the question "What does the president do all day?" weren't so different when I questioned inner-city seven-year-olds.

❖❖❖ "He works in a square office, I think, counting money."

❖❖❖ "He just signs papers other people make up."

❖❖❖ "He visits everybody who comes to the White House."

In most kindergarten classes I was surprised to discover how few of the feminist ideas had managed to trickle down.

Question: What does the president's wife do all day?

❖❖❖ "Her nails?"

By far the most frequent response was "Cooks."

❖❖❖ "She has to cook all day long because the president usually has a lot of friends from different countries over for dinner."

❖❖❖ "She cooks the president's breakfast, lunch, and dinner every day."

The second most common response was "She cleans."

❖❖❖ "She cleans the whole house white, the White House."

❖❖❖ "She has to scrub up the kitchen at nights."

And she was assigned other domestic duties as well:

❖❖❖ "She knits."

❖❖❖ "She sews his clothes."

❖❖❖ "She has to raise the kids almost all by herself because the president hardly ever sees them because he's gone so much."

❖❖❖ "She has to help everybody with their homework."

❖❖❖ "She tries to get the president to move."

"Why does she want to move?"

"That's an awful big house for only two people."

❖❖❖ "I know what she does all day," said an inner-city first-grade girl. "She just sits around all day being rich. And she has her own TV in her own bedroom."

❖❖❖ One first-grader had a different idea of the president's wife. "She waits for him to die."

"She waits for the president to die?" I asked, shocked.

"Well," he continued, "if he dies, then she gets to be president."

But his buddy disagreed. "No sir. If the president dies, then the vice president gets to be president."

"Oh, that's right," the first boy had to admit. "So they both wait until the president dies."

Question: Do you think we should have a woman president of the United States?

❖❖❖ I asked a panel of three girls and two boys. All of them giggled, especially the girls.

"Why are you laughing?" I asked. "Don't you think it's a good idea to have a woman president?"

"You can't have a woman for president," one of the girls told me firmly.

"Why not?"

"Because she has to be the wife."

But a second girl changed her mind. "No, yeah. A lady could be president and her husband could be the president's wife."

Question: Why have we never had a woman president of the United States?

❖❖❖ "Because girls aren't smart enough," Albert was quick to say.

"Girls are smarter than boys," Latissa protested. "Boys just aren't smart enough to vote for girls."

❖❖❖ "None of us ever wanted to be one before," said a first-grade girl.

❖❖❖ "We haven't?" was the response of one kindergarten gal.

"No, we haven't," I assured her.

She sighed. "Life is so unfair. My brother gets to be on a flag football team, and I don't. So I know how it feels."

Question: What does a vice president do?

❖❖❖ "He helps the president stay healthy."

❖❖❖ "He listens to the president and the president's wife."

❖❖❖ "He just practices being president."

"How does he do that?"

"He looks at himself in a mirror and tries to talk like the president and move his arms like the president and everything. Then if the real president dies, he can jump in and nobody won't notice he's not real."

❖❖❖ "When the president doesn't show up for work, they let the vice president do it."

Question: What could a president do that would be bad enough to get him fired?

❖❖❖ "Do drugs."

❖❖❖ "He could have a party for drug dealers, with drinking. And then if the governors catch him, they'd fire him."

❖❖❖ "If he ran over people with a train, he could get fired."

❖❖❖ "He could rob a bank. Would they fire you if you robbed a bank?"

❖❖❖ "He could throw some kid who didn't know how to swim into the White House swimming pool. Then he'd really get fired."

❖❖❖ "They might fire him if he stopped working. But I don't know for sure."

❖❖❖ "He could stab somebody. Or shoot the vice president."

Question: What's the biggest problem the president faces?

❖❖❖ "How to give talks on TV and not look scared."

❖❖❖ "How to keep his friends from getting jealous."

❖❖❖ "Fire. That's about the biggest problem."

❖❖❖ "Mud."

"Mud?" I asked, feeling the need to clarify the answer. "The biggest problem the president of the United States has is mud?"

"Yes. Mud at the White House."

"Why is that?" I asked.

"Well, if it's too muddy there, he can't go outside. And if he's outside and it gets muddy, then he can't go back inside the White House. So he's stuck either way."

❖❖❖ "Taxes," a seven-year-old boy answered with confidence.

"Taxes?" I repeated. "What are taxes?"

"It's a really big state where all the mean cowboys live."

❖❖❖ "His biggest problem is watching himself every time he shows up on TV because he's really boring. And then he has to watch the news and weather every single day. That's his biggest problem."

Question: What would you do if you were president of the United States?

❖❖❖ "I'd tell everybody to give away all their money and I'd make everything free. You couldn't even pay if you wanted to. And we'd make deliveries for free to the homeless."

❖❖❖ "I'd collect all the money in taxes," said Robert.

"That wouldn't make you a very popular president," I told him.

"But then," he continued, "I'd take all the money up in my helicopter and throw it around the world evenly."

❖❖❖ "I'd clean up the earth."

"How would you manage that?"

"Easy. I'd let all the gas out of cars while nobody was looking."

"But what about all the other gas?" I asked.

"I'd hide it all in the Statue of Liberty," she said assuredly.

"Why the Statue of Liberty?"

"Who would ever think to look there for it?"

❖❖❖ "I wouldn't let there be any drugs," claimed an inner-city third-grader.

"How do you think you'd do that?" protested his classmate.

"I'd have all the policemen dress up like drug dealers and all the police stations dress up like drug houses. Then I'd change all the druggies I arrested."

"How can one person do all that?" challenged his friend.

"Oh, I wouldn't be able to do it overnight. I'd take my time and not rush it. If it took me a week or a month, I wouldn't give up."

❖❖❖ "If I were president, I'd take it easy and relax and make about $1005 before I was through."

❖❖❖ "Huh-uh," said Anita, shaking her head and holding up her hands. "You couldn't make me be president even if you elected me. I wouldn't do it."

"Why not?" I asked.

"There's nothing to do. The world's already ruined."

✹ *CHAPTER 13* ✹

If I Ruled the World

Almost everything that is great has been done by youth.—Benjamin Disraeli

Question: What would you children change if you got to rule the world?

❖❖❖ "Desserts would be main meals and spinach and veggies would be for dessert, only if you wanted them."

❖❖❖ "You couldn't be president unless you had candy to give everyone."

❖❖❖ "Girls could be president too."

❖❖❖ "Everything would cost one penny, except for poor people. They'd get everything free."

❖❖❖ "We'd make parents go to bed early."

❖❖❖ "We'd have babies be born knowing everything and not needing school. Then as you got older, you'd forget some of the stuff you were born knowing; and so you'd have to ask a kid."

❖❖❖ "We'd stop all wars. And anyone who started war again would have to be dunked in a tub of lemonade."

Question: What do parents need to know?

❖❖❖ "They need to know where Colorado is on the map."

❖❖❖ "They need to believe their kids when their kids say they're sick. And then they need to know how to find a doctor."

❖❖❖ "They ought to learn how to get gum out of kids' hair without pulling out the hair."

❖❖❖ "They need to remember the rule 'If something is living, leave it alone.'"

❖❖❖ "They should tell their kids not to go into their parents' rooms because their dads might have books with bad stuff in them."

❖❖❖ "Never leave babies in cars with the windows closed."

❖❖❖ "Buy a newspaper that has cartoons in it every day."

❖❖❖ "Don't let your kids have BB guns and shoot themselves in the forehead."

❖❖❖ "If you lose your son in the mall, you can find him in the lost and found."

❖❖❖ "Don't just teach little girls to cook. Teach your little boys to cook too."

❖❖❖ "Don't smoke because it goes into your kid's stomach."

❖❖❖ "Save the rain forests."

❖❖❖ "Stop being pushy and perfect."

❖❖❖ "Treat us like you want to be treated. And that means give us a break."

❖❖❖ "Don't cut down trees."

❖❖❖ "Get glasses so you can see kids better!"

❖❖❖ "Get a grip on it!"

❖❖❖ "Get a life!"

❖❖❖ "Pick on someone your own size."

I happened onto a class of second-graders who were undertaking a goodwill project. Each child composed a personal greeting, enclosed it in a balloon, filled the balloon with helium, and set it aloft to carry goodwill across the country as far as the balloon would sail. Imagine being on the receiving end of some of these messages:

❖❖❖ "My name is Kathy. What's yours? I hope you like this balloon. I wanted to keep it, but my teacher wouldn't let me."

❖❖❖ "Dear whoever gets this. You are invited to my birthday party on May 26. Do you like chocolate cake with green icing? . . . P.S. Don't tell my mom about the party."

❖❖❖ "If this ends up in Alaska, please send me some snow. It never snows here."

❖❖❖ "I bet Brad ______ that my balloon would go farther than his balloon. So if you're not very far away, will you please blow this up again and give it another push?"

❖❖❖ "My dog died yesterday. Love, Philip."

❖❖❖ "I'm in the second grade, and I'm drug-free."

Today's kids have heard all about drugs. When I asked "What are drugs?" I didn't receive a single "I don't know."

Question: What are drugs?

❖❖❖ "They're things that fry your brain."

❖❖❖ "Things that kill you."

❖❖❖ "Drugs are medicine that's deadly if you're not sick."

❖❖❖ "It's like when you're chubby and you take your whole bottle of diet pills and go to the hospital."

❖❖❖ "Drugs are pills, marijuana, wine, beer, smoking, and anything you do every day."

❖❖❖ "Things that make you drunk or dead."

❖❖❖ "They make you plop in bed if you take over two of them."

❖❖❖ "My dad smokes drugs and it gives him brown teeth."

❖❖❖❖❖❖

Question: Do you have a wish for the world?

❖❖❖ "World peace, and no littering."

❖❖❖ "I wish they'd pick a woman for president."

❖❖❖ "I wish they'd remember that women may not be strong on the outside, but they are strong inside."

❖❖❖ "Work smart, not hard."

❖❖❖ "I wish my telephone had all sixes in it. Then it would be easier to remember."

❖❖❖ "I wish everybody would stop selling drugs."

❖❖❖ "My wish for the world would be no more war, no one using drugs—and everyone's perm should turn out nicely."

One teacher sent me "Words to Live By," prepared by her sixth-grade class. Here are a few of their tips, advice from kids to kids:

❖❖❖ "The earth cannot be wasted by those of us who need it."

❖❖❖ "Don't expect your older brothers or sisters to keep secrets."

❖❖❖ "Never go on a Tilt-a-Wheel right after lunch."

❖❖❖ "Your mom doesn't like saying something more than twice."

❖❖❖ "Don't forget to close the door behind you."

❖❖❖ "You can't get ink poisoning by writing on your hand, or I'd be dead."

❖❖❖ "Never assume your mother won't mind it if you leave something lying around when you tell her you'll pick it up later."

❖❖❖ "You can't buy self-control in the supermarket."

❖❖❖ "Don't pull. Push."

❖❖❖ "Whoever said it doesn't matter if you win or lose never played sports."

❖❖❖ "If you don't make the team, you can always be the water boy."

❖❖❖ "Instead of putting the kid in the playpen, put the Christmas tree in the playpen."

❖❖❖ "When your younger brother or sister starts walking, move your valuables a few feet higher."

❖❖❖ "Tell your parents not to get you a brother or sister until you get an eleven-year head start."

❖❖❖ "Don't forget to let the toilet seat down."

❖❖❖ "Nothing happens if people don't cooperate."

Question: Do you have any last words of advice for all grown-ups everywhere?

❖❖❖ "Don't try to kill yourselves."

❖❖❖ "Don't get ran over."

❖❖❖ "If you see bad people, say NO and call the police."

❖❖❖ "If your kids tell you they have a meeting at school, don't forget it. They want you to go to stuff."

❖❖❖ "Stop watching TV all night! You'd be better off going to bed when your kids do. You can read books too, you know."

❖❖❖ "Get out of the city while there's still time!"

❖❖❖ "Love each other, even if you're divorced."

❖❖❖ "Don't steal cars or limos."

❖❖❖ "People in Africa need food."

❖❖❖ "Children need to play every day."

❖❖❖ "Recycle!"

❖❖❖ "Watch your billfolds."

❖❖❖ "Don't get divorced."

❖❖❖ "Don't eat cigarettes."

❖❖❖ "Don't take whiskey."

❖❖❖ "Don't take tobacco."

❖❖❖ "Don't date women under thirty-one."

❖❖❖ "Don't forget to water your trees."

❖❖❖ "Don't smoke while you're reading (or doing anything else)."

❖❖❖ "Don't eat pills when you don't have a cold."

❖❖❖ "Don't eat drugs and forget how to read."

❖❖❖ "Don't wear shorts in the winter."

❖❖❖ "Don't let kids chew gum while they're sleeping."

❖❖❖ "Don't let two-year-olds kiss three-year-olds on the lips."

❖❖❖ "Don't smoke while you're making babies."

❖❖❖ "Don't spank. Just yell."

❖❖❖ "Don't make your kids run away."

❖❖❖ "Don't let kids mess with bleach."

❖❖❖ "Don't take candy from strangers—even if you know them."

❖❖❖ "Don't kill innocent animals."

❖❖❖ "Don't eat bugs."

❖❖❖ "Don't ignore your children."

Index